TRACING YOUR
LEGAL
ANCESTORS

TRACING YOUR LEGAL ANCESTORS

A GUIDE FOR FAMILY HISTORIANS

Stephen Wade

Pen & Sword
FAMILY HISTORY

First published in Great Britain in 2010 by
PEN & SWORD FAMILY HISTORY
an imprint of
Pen & Sword Books Ltd
47 Church Street
Barnsley
South Yorkshire
S70 2AS

Copyright © Stephen Wade 2010

ISBN 978 1 84884 226 7

The right of Stephen Wade to be identified as Author of this Work has been
asserted by him in accordance with the Copyright,
Designs and Patents Act 1988.

A CIP catalogue record for this book is
available from the British Library.

Typeset in Palatino and Optima by
Phoenix Typesetting, Auldgirth, Dumfriesshire

Printed and bound in England by
CPI UK

Pen & Sword Books Ltd incorporates the imprints of
Pen & Sword Aviation, Pen & Sword Maritime, Pen & Sword Military,
Wharncliffe Local History, Pen and Sword Select, Pen and Sword Military
Classics, Leo Cooper, Remember When, Seaforth Publishing and
Frontline Publishing.

For a complete list of Pen & Sword titles please contact
PEN & SWORD BOOKS LIMITED
47 Church Street, Barnsley, South Yorkshire, S70 2AS, England
E-mail: enquiries@pen-and-sword.co.uk
Website: www.pen-and-sword.co.uk

CONTENTS

ACKNOWLEDGEMENTS

Assembling the material for this book from so many diverse and often ephemeral sources has meant that professional help has been required. Thanks go particularly to Adrian Wilkinson at the Lincolnshire Archives, staff at the University of Hull Brynmor Jones Library, and to several scholars who have paid attention to obscure footnotes in the history of law and the legal profession. One curiosity was the discovery of a history of Staple Inn, with manuscript notes and additions in my copy of *Staple Inn and its Story*, by T Cato Worsfold: I owe him or her thanks. I have also spoken to various retired lawyers and they have been invaluable in helping a mere layman and enthusiast to grasp some of the intricacies of the law machine.

Preparation has meant much trawling through archives, sending online queries to experts and generally asking obscure questions of a range of specialists. This must necessarily happen when a mere historian sets himself the task of explaining some areas of the law. The sources have been diverse and very mixed, so help was needed all along the way, and it has been no mean task to compile this volume with the lay reader in mind. I have tried to add contextual depth where needed, to explain certain statutes and changes in the law where this will help the researcher into family history.

Specific thanks go to Lincolnshire County Council, County Archives, for permission to use the documents from the Peake, Snow and Jeudwine files (PSJ 12F/A/8) and quarter sessions materials (4 BM/19/8/4/6). Also to the ground-breaking first work on the subject, *My Ancestor was a Lawyer*, by Brian Brooks and Mark Herber.

Thanks are due to the Welsh Legal History Society, and specifically to Richard Ireland. The illustration here from Brecon is by permission of Richard W Ireland/Welsh History Society.

Simon Fowler was a great help in pointing out the necessity of recasting the format of the book, and so thanks go to him for that assistance.

Finally, the great doyen of English legal history, JH Baker, stands behind this book, as he does behind most writing on the history of the legal professions, and before him, FW Maitland. Baker's work across journals and in his major works will always be worth checking if the researcher is going back beyond the Reformation, and particularly for barrister ancestors.

HOW TO USE THIS BOOK

There is no doubt that understanding the history of the legal profession is a complex business. The terms used for the various positions and offices are couched in a specific professional vocabulary often relating to microcosms of the lawyer's rather hermetically sealed spheres of activity. For that reason, I have had to mix explanations of the law itself, the terminology integral to the profession, and social factors linked to the changing roles and identities of legal professionals through time.

I recommend, with this in mind, that the reader absorbs the historical factors in the first two chapters and the introduction, and then proceeds via the index to locate the specific occupation of the ancestor. Basically, understanding what the 'job description' was at a particular time is the answer to the problem raised by the language barrier in the various texts in which sources of information are found is the secret of success.

Most space is devoted to barristers, solicitors, notaries and the most prominent clerks. In addition, because there have been so many courts over the centuries, changing as new legislation came along and sometimes being abolished, I have devoted a large portion of the book to explanations of the courts. This is essential, just as understanding a Victorian farm would entail a whole range of jobs, trades and professions, many of which are now long gone.

To summarise, because the law is a closed book to many, and any attempt to understand it by a layman is bound to be a formidable prospect, the process of discovery needs to be simplified. Therefore, follow these steps:

1 Start with the understanding of the vocabulary related to the ancestor as far as is known – position, legal work etc
2 Gather and list potential sources from the period
3 Add to the basic biographical facts
4 Then move on to the most time-consuming part – going to archives and searching for the less easily accessible material.

Here is an example. Let us suppose the ancestor was a solicitor in c.1890.

1 Be sure of the language pinned to his work: 'conveyancing' for instance

2 Sources: starting with *The Law List* and almanacs, his address, date of admission and address of firm would be ascertained

3 Search the digital archives and press reports for any references to him. For instance, the author of the history of Staples Inn, described in chapter 2, T Cato Worsfold, is listed in ten references in *The Times* Digital Archive, some accounts merely listing his attendance at events but others giving paragraphs on his talks or involvement in cases, or even his official positions such as his advisory work with organisations.

4 Then comes the more demanding business of trawling archives such as company materials at the County Record Office. Depending on the dates in which he was active, there may be firms' records, although they may present fairly dull material in the case of a country solicitor. Nevertheless, the person is *your* ancestor.

TRACING YOUR LEGAL ANCESTORS

INTRODUCTION

The professions explained

Most people are only too happy to have very little to do with the law in their lives. Legal professionals may only affect our lives when we need conveyancing done or when a will has to be drawn up. Civil law therefore is almost certain to play some part in ordinary lives; criminal law is quite another thing – an institution best kept well away, a source of fear and trepidation. But what about all the various professionals who administrate law in all its forms? Arguably, the lay person knows very little indeed about them and what they do.

Britain has always had a proliferation of names for legal people. In the USA there is no distinction between lawyers who act as advocates in court – our barristers – and the everyday solicitor. Americans use the word 'attorney' for all roles. But in Britain, we have barristers and solicitors, and that is just the beginning.

The enquiry into legal profession ancestors necessarily entails a confrontation with a number of sources which present the kind of knowledge that tends to gather around regulatory groups and circumscribed areas of expertise. In other words, there will be a need to penetrate the general obfuscation of language around an elite, or an exclusive group. To put it simply, without an understanding of the rituals and traditions of the legal professions, the task of the family historian is much harder. Every document and source will have its almost 'coded' form and language. But even above that, there is the plain fact that the main legal professions have very long histories and that fact has meant that the changing face of their work and training has meant that the context of the research will always be essential to know. This book will incorporate those elements of the subject, as a preface to each category of record. The glossary at the end of the main text will supplement that.

The history of lawyers and their subsidiary workers begins with a range of amateurs: people who would speak for others in a trial. In classical times, in Greece and Rome, steadily the professional lawyer emerged from a number of high-class, articulate people who would advise on the law. By the third century BC there were clearly professional lawyers working in Rome, as an act of 204 BC forbade advocates from taking fees. The legal professional was simply an advocate (someone speaking for or pleading for, someone else). But gradually professionals appeared, giving legal opinions on current issues; by the first century the professionalisation was complete, and there were then notaries, advocates and legal advisers. In England, as will be seen in chapter 2, it was not until the mid-twelfth century that legal experts appeared. Then, the medieval church was of course very powerful, and ecclesiastical courts were the training grounds of the men who acted as professionals: after all, they knew Latin and had studied rhetoric (the art of argumentation and persuasive speaking).

Throughout our legal history, the British have had hundreds of legal occupations, all describing very specific roles and duties. Most of these have attracted jokes and a degree of cynicism. The great poet Chaucer, writing around 1390, has a lawyer among his pilgrims travelling to Canterbury and he says, 'Though there was none so busy as was he/ he was less busy than he seemed to be.' That would certainly not apply today, as great upheavals in lawyers' lives and fees are taking place. But there has been a need to give the law and lawyers a more approachable and open public image, to counteract this poor reputation. In 1988 a Law Society spokesman said, 'We must change our image. We must be seen as champions of justice, not parasites which feed on it.'

In 2009, barristers were embroiled in all kinds of reforms and revisions of their profession. *The Times* in November 2009, for instance, reported that Husnara Begum, who uses a wheelchair and has rheumatoid arthritis, won a contract to work with a top law firm. She told the press that the lack of white working-class men or Afro-Caribbeans in the law can be blamed on education rather than prejudice. 'Mentoring and encouragement of these groups should start much earlier, at school . . . if these youngsters don't get into a good university, they will have little chance of a legal career.' In other words, although the world has changed radically since the Victorian period, when barristers were a very special elite indeed, it is still tough to reach a high status in the legal professions.

Researching your legal profession ancestor demands an understanding of what the various occupations were, from barristers' clerks to coroners, and from magistrates to solicitors; but it also needs a knowledge of legal terminology and the structures of the legal system in order that the ancestor's work and status may be understood. The records themselves are also, on the surface, quite formidable. There have been so many courts throughout the centuries, and so many varieties of vocabulary used (often in Latin) that it is a challenge to get to grips with the ancestor's daily chores and duties.

For instance, in chapter 6 my case study is of a family of solicitors in Lincolnshire, and the archival material contains a large number of professional documents, covering apprenticeship indentures to settlements of estates. In addition, archives often have various books and publications relating to law work: solicitors have always had yearbooks, diaries, appointment books, payment books for fees and so on. Therefore, despite the daunting task of looking for your ancestor among the hundreds of categories in the records, the good news is that the documentation is solid and varied.

The first step is to have some definitions of most of the main professions. This checklist is to introduce the occupations and their roles through history. First, to understand the diversity of occupations, a look at *The British Almanac* for 1836 gives some notion of the range of legal workers then. The 'miscellaneous register' in that volume includes: four titles in the Court of Chancery; five titles in the ecclesiastical courts; titles of roles in the courts of Admiralty, Bankruptcy, Insolvent Debtors' Court, the Marshalsea and Palace Courts, the Courts of Requests; Lord Lieutenants of England and Wales; administrators for all courts, and judges at quarter sessions and assize courts. This, for example, is the listing under 'Court of Session':

COURT OF SESSION
First Division
The Lord President: Ch. Hope
DWR Ewart and other judges
Permanent ordinaries: Geo. Cranstoun, Lord Corehouse, John Fullerton
Ordinary on the Bills and Teinds: Lord Cockburn
Principal Clerks: A. Bolland, Geo. Bell

In the second court there were more permanent ordinaries and principal clerks. Then in the same year there were in the Court of Exchequer these offices: Baron, King's Remembrancer, Auditor, Lord Advocate, Solicitor-General, advocates depute, crown agent, clerk of justiciary. In the Middle Temple, one of the Inns of Court where lawyers were trained, there were nine official posts. It may be seen from this that official legal positions proliferated, as there were so many courts and legal institutions at the time. Many occupations have long gone, such as the office of 'proctor, a post roughly equivalent to that of solicitor, but referring to the person functioning in the Ecclesiastical, Admiralty, Divorce and Matrimonial Courts'. Many of the medieval terms have, of course, disappeared. But it is essential to have some knowledge of these when searching records. Sometimes, the printed primary sources have explanations of these offices, as in the memoirs discussed in chapter 7.

Checklist of main legal professions/occupations

Attorney In the widest sense, this refers to a person who acts in place of another. Then the term was used to describe people who practised in the superior courts of common law.

Barrister A barrister is a member of one of the four Inns of Court (see chapter 2) who is called to the Bar. The Bar was originally a bench where senior lawyers sat in debate. Mainly, barristers advise, represent clients and draft statements of cases. They are supervised by the General Council of the Bar of England and Wales.

Barrister's Clerk This clerk leads the administration process of the work of a barrister. They will tend to be involved in the business of organising briefs and being intermediaries where required.

Clerk of Assize The main official administrating at assize courts (abolished in 1971)

Clerks of the Common Pleas The Court of Common Pleas was linked to the sovereign's court, the *Curia Regis*, which by the Judicature Act of 1873 was transferred to the High Court of Justice. The clerk officiated there.

Common Lawyers These were best defined and explained by the Elizabethan writer, John Stow, who wrote that in London there was 'a whole university . . . of students, practicers [sic] or pleaders, and judges of the laws of this realm, not living on common stipends, as in other universities . . . but of their own private maintenance . . . for that the younger sort are either gentlemen or the sons of gentlemen'.

Conciliar Courts Staff The new courts created under the Tudors also formed new titles and positions, among them the clerks of the Star Chamber courts, and there were various others with special responsibilities such as 'the attorney of the court of wards'. When reading records from the late Victorian years back to the Reformation, researchers will note a proliferation of these posts.

Conveyancer Deeds of conveyance are very ancient indeed: Anglo-Saxon charters and church *scriptoria* (studies where manuscripts were written and copied) demanded educated men to work there and, over time, a professional body emerged; and from c.1350 there were scriveners who wrote legal documents. As Alan Harding stated in 1966, 'A conveyancer needed to be expert in the law which determined the validity of his products.' In 1641 a publication called *A Touchstone of Common Assurances* noted the universality of 'an unlearned and yet pragmatical attorney or a lawless scrivener . . . or an ignorant vicar . . . and yet who is apt and liable . . . to make a conveyance'.

Judge The judge is the legal official who sits in judgement in the courts of the realm; in the past they fell into different categories such as circuit judges for the assizes, or appeal judges for appeal courts.

Justice's Clerk The main legal adviser to the bench of magistrates. One practitioner, Ernest Pettifer, explained the role in this way: 'He is in a strange position, for, although he is there to advise his justices upon the law of each case, he has no authority to enforce his opinion, and the justices can disregard his views.'

Magistrate The magistrate is a justice of the peace, dealing with summary criminal cases (hearings without a jury). Historically, as JPs, they sat on the bench in their local area, and were usually land-owners or clerics.

Master of the Rolls This is the President of the Civil Division of the Court of Appeal. After the 1881 Judicature Act the post was applied also to the role as judge of the Court of Appeal. In the reign of Elizabeth I he was also a privy councillor.

Narrators In the early thirteenth century, this term was used for the person who spoke for litigants at the King's Court.

Notary Mainly, an official who attests deeds and who produces copies of documents. 'It is the office of a notary, amongst other things, at the request of the holder of a bill of exchange, of which acceptance or payment is refused, to note a bill.' *Mozley and Whiteley's Law Dictionary.*

Proctor A person who is selected to represent a collegiate or church in the lower house of convocation; also a representative who defends a suit for another person.

Queen's/King's Counsel Barristers who are appointed to be Counsel to the Queen (formerly the King). They are often referred to as 'silks' as they wear silk gowns, and they take precedence over junior barristers.

Recorder The main legal officer of a city or town. In that office, the person may sit as a judge in any county court district.

Scrivener In the legal context, this was a person who drew up contracts. From the *Scrivener's Company Common Paper*, covering the years 1357–1628, we have an oath given to a scrivener on admission to his profession. Part of it reads: ' . . . there will be no untruth felt in my conscience and I will make no copy of any deed sealed . . . and I shall not take upon me any act touching upon inheritance nor any other act of great charge . . . ' In other words, they were being kept in their place, as 'inferior to attorneys'.

Serjeant By 1310 the term 'serjeant-at-law' was being used for people who gave counsel to their masters, and could be retained to argue cases in the Common Pleas. 'The serjeants were the people who specialized in the substance of legal disputes.' (Alan Harding) The title was abolished in 1877.

Solicitor This is a broadly applied name for a person who advises on legal matters and supervises legal proceedings. He or she will have a certificate issued by the Law Society. In 2004, over 96,000 solicitors in Britain had certificates licensing them to practise.

An overview of sources

As will be explained in chapter 5, the central resource for tracing legal profession ancestors is in a number of categories of archives in The National Archives (TNA). These materials cover judges and serjeants, barristers, solicitors and attorneys in the central courts; and solicitors and attorneys in the Palatinate Courts of Chester, Durham and Lancaster. In addition there are the Welsh courts, then civil lawyers. The Law Society also has some records.

To complement this, tracing these ancestors involves an exploration of a range of newspaper and journal sources, and there has always been detailed reporting in national papers of activities by lawyers of all kinds. There are also reference works such as almanacs and year-books; professional publications such as law reports, and sources in County Record Offices. The latter topic opens up a vast amount of information because there are often extensive records of family businesses in particular in the regional archives.

One exceptionally useful aspect of records of legal ancestors is that naturally there have always been extensive reporting and translations of courts and trials from all kinds of sources, so there will be openings to develop a fuller narrative of an ancestor's life in materials ranging from state papers and parliamentary papers to quarter sessions records. Learned societies and record societies have also been busy for some time in translating earlier court records such as pleas, assizes and rolls from manorial courts, so it is not such a difficult task in some cases to trace the ancestor back to times before the eighteenth century, when records in English began in criminal materials, for example.

Professional bodies

It is also very useful to know something of the influential professional bodies in the law, and here it is necessary to describe the English organisations; the Irish and Scottish equivalents will be explained in the relevant chapters later.

The Bar Council

This is the body that regulates the Bar, properly known as the General Council of the Bar of England and Wales. It was founded in 1894 to represent the interests of barristers, and it works with the Inns of Court on matters of professional concern.

Guilds

These are fraternities relating to trades and professions, and their authority is from a royal charter, and in London the notion of a guild as a livery company dates back to 1560. The aldermen of the City of London, acting in courts, and scriveners, for instance, would be instances of legal professionals belonging to guilds.

The Inns of Court

This term refers to the group of four inns in London: the Middle Temple, Inner Temple, Lincoln's Inn and Gray's Inn. Established in the fourteenth century, they are not subject to the jurisdiction of the courts, but are voluntary associations. Their most important function is that they have a monopoly on the process of calling legal professionals to the Bar.

The Law Society

The basic division of barristers on the one hand and attorneys and solicitors on the other had been established by the Tudor period; estates, wills and settlements were the province of the latter and representations in lawsuits defined the province of the former. After the steady development of important aspects of trial procedure, interested parties from legal professionals created what was first called The London Institution in 1823 and their aim was to make proper professional standards of behaviour and qualification. Two years later it was re-named the Law Society, coming into being on 2 June 1825, then being given a royal charter in 1831. Although it was properly called The Society of Attorneys, Solicitors, Proctors and others not being Barristers practising in the Courts of Law and Equity in the United Kingdom, it was the Law Society in common parlance. The headquarters was established in Chancery Lane, and in 1845 it was made an independent society, supervising the legal profession.

In 1922 women were admitted as members, and that meant the end of a long and persistent struggle on the part of female scholars at universities to win entry to the very conservative profession of the law, and in particular, the Bar.

One of the main concerns was regulation and standards. As early as 1834 the Law Society began proceedings against legal officials who were falling short and who slipped into criminal behaviour; a committee was formed to control the instruments of regulation. But there has always been an educative element too, with lectures being given in the Hall of the Society, dating back to 1835. In 1903 the Society created its own School of Law, and even today, the Society still validates legal education and other elements of professional training.

There had been provision for some kind of law training even as far back as the late twelfth century, but in 1234 Henry III wanted to remove the schools; his proclamation was: 'That through the whole of the city of London let it be proclaimed and wholly forbidden that anyone who has a school for law in that town shall teach the laws inter alia, and if anyone shall conduct a school of that nature there, the mayor and sheriffs shall put a stop to it at once.'

A survey of the courts system

If your ancestor was a 'black sheep' who fell foul of the law, or if he or she merely offended the local church in some small way, they could have been destined for a court appearance. For researching family history it is essential to have a grasp of which courts were important and where their records are. What complicates matters is that through the centuries, a crime could have been dealt with in manorial courts, summary courts or church courts. There were even special courts for the Army and for the Admiralty. Your ancestor's offence therefore leaves a paper trail but that might run through a dark forest rather than a sunlit path.

The important point to keep in mind for present purposes is that the names of legal professionals were usually there in many records, and in fact in the editions produced by societies such as the Chetham Society and others, there are indexes of names.

The Chetham Society specialises in producing records relating to the North West of England, and their publications include various texts of a legal nature, including court records and notebooks of lawyers. Much of the material is biographical, but there are also such items as a Calendar of County Court and Eyre Rolls of Chester 1259–1297 and Court Leet Records for the manor of Manchester in the Sixteenth Century. (See the bibliography for full details.) These publications date back to the time the Society was founded in 1843.

Offences

First be clear about this distinction: **Summary** and **indictable.** A summary offence may be tried by a magistrate only, whereas an indictable offence has to be tried before a jury. This relates also to the definitions of *felony* and *misdemeanour*: a felony, until the Criminal Law Act of 1967, was a serious offence, and before 1870, it meant that the convict would forfeit all lands and chattels, and was often sentenced to death as well. A misdemeanour was a less extreme offence, usually tried summarily.

Medieval courts

In the centuries between the Anglo-Saxon kingdoms and the first assizes (courts on a national circuit held by the King's travelling justices) before there were proper courts there was a system of blood-price and hue and cry. The local hundreds, groups of people, would be responsible for law and order in their communities. More serious crimes were dealt with by ordeals of water or fire. But with the manors and the bishoprics came manorial and church courts and after them, in 1361, the justices of the peace, the magistrates.

The records of these early courts are in Latin, but many have been translated by county record societies and are available in printed form. For more serious offences – felonies – the most common sentences are fines and outlawry. Fines gave the sovereign money, whereas a hanging yielded him nothing. As for outlaws, they were hounded by everyone and their fate was almost always a bloody death, with all their possessions forfeited.

All this was before the reforms of the fourteenth and fifteenth centuries when 'The King's Peace' was more thoroughly preserved in a series of statutes. For the family historian, this means that records from before the Tudor period present the problem of having to cope with legal language which is notably difficult to construe. But the statutes relating to the 'King's Peace' – records of the main courts in London and to the *eyre* court (the first courts held on a circuit across the land) – are gradually being made available with notes and explanations of terms.

The powerful bishops could and did hang felons, so most areas, as may be seen on old large-scale maps, had gallows dotted around, some secular and some ecclesiastical. All this was before the reforms of the fourteenth and fifteenth centuries when 'The King's Peace' was more thoroughly preserved in a series of statutes.

Early Modern courts

Throughout the centuries, small misdemeanours were dealt with quickly and efficiently in manorial court leets or other kinds of summary courts. As Peter King has written in his study of these courts, 'In almost every county there were also many magistrates who heard individual cases alone in their homes' and he notes that, 'an increasing number of both administrative and legal functions were passed down to them by the legislature . . . ' We can have a glimpse at this kind of record if we look at *The Justicing Notebook of Edmund Tew, Rector of Bolden*, published by the Surtees Society. In his journal we find entries such as these:

1763
November 15th. Granted general warrant against Isabel Reed of Shields, fruiterer, for defrauding . . . of ditto widow a pair of shoes. Agreed.
22th Granted a search warrant against George Turner of

Jarrow, farmer, for concealing timber in his outhouse of Robert Waynman of North Shields. Agreed.

For various areas of the North East and the North West of England, the publications of the Chetham Society and the Surtees Society provide a great deal of details of offenders in those areas in the Early Modern period, and in fact, the court leet records of Manchester for the sixteenth century give a very substantial account of such legal practices. A court leet was a type of summary court, probably coming from the Old English verb *gelethian*, to assemble together. Manchester ancestors who transgressed even in these very minor ways can be located in the records and indexes of the printed volumes, as in the Chetham Society editions.

These sources show just what a huge amount of everyday law was handled by the magistrates and the justices presiding at leets and petty sessions. The topics coming before the sessions could be anything from petty theft to homicide, but much of the time was taken up with sorting out people from other parishes who had come into another parish, or with lack of payment to constables. Often it was a matter of debating issues such as who should repair a certain bridge or what should be done with a deserter. With every day that passes, more and more of these texts are made available, and are often found in university libraries as well as in local archives.

Particularly useful in this context is Robert Burlison's book, *Tracing Your Pauper Ancestors* (see bibliography).

The Modern period, Victorian to the end of Assizes

Most of the courts structure for both civil and criminal cases concerned these institutions:

Assizes

These were held from the thirteenth century until 1971. The system had its origins in a court in which two judges would hold the sovereign's court twice a year. These tried criminal and civil cases. From 1550 records provide details of such offences as homicide, infanticide and major theft. Before 1733 assize records are in Latin and the main records are indictments (statements of charges); depositions (written evidences) and gaol books or minutes (lists of accused persons and summaries of cases heard). If there are no assize records surviving, then there are sheriffs' assize vouchers, located at TNA E389 and also, for writs, in the King's Bench records.

The Gentleman's Magazine published details of the assize circuits, such as this entry from the 1819 issue: 'Spring Circuits, 1819, Norfolk, Lord Chief Justice Abbott and Baron Graham; Aylesbury, March 4, Bedford March 10, Huntingdon March 13, Thetford, March 20, Bury St Edmunds, March 26.'

Quarter Sessions

These were courts where justices of the peace sat in judgement, from their creation in 1285. By the eighteenth century these 'bench' meetings had a massive workload because there had been a great deal of voluminous statute law created by successive Hanoverian governments, mainly relating to offences against property and persons: the result, in part, of there being no professional police force.

Petty Sessions

These were summary courts, dealing with all kinds of minor matters, normally with two magistrates sitting. From 1828 quarter sessions were empowered to form petty sessions. Increasingly, in the Victorian period, police courts took over the handling of everyday criminal proceedings. The simplest way to understand what these were and how they worked is to search *The Times* Digital Archive for such as 'Hull Police Court' and study some examples. In addition, there is also the British Library digitised nineteenth-century newspapers project; on the British Newspapers 1800–1900 resource for instance, there are two million pages of newspaper material to search, covering both local and national publications.

In the 1850s, Charles Dickens edited a journal called *Household Narrative* (a monthly supplement to his *Household Words*). In this publication we find summary reports under the heading 'Law and Crime' and a glance at the 1854 collected volumes has reports from these courts: a court-martial; Lincolnshire assizes; the London

Guildhall; Bow Street Magistrates' Court; Marlborough Street Police Court; a coroner's inquest at Hunslet (Leeds), and the Court of Queen's Bench sitting in Dublin. Criminal ancestors were present in all these locations, with crimes ranging from 'stealing a bit of velvet riband' to a case of 'wilful murder against Joseph Baines' who was charged with killing his wife. Such is the proliferation of courts and trials in British history and the family historian needs to find a way through this labyrinth.

The Georgian and Victorian years saw first a rise in capital crimes, up to c.1820, and then a gradual dominance of police courts and magistrates' courts to sort out less serious offences, while quarter sessions and assizes dealt with almost everything. But in 1861 the Offences Against the Persons Act reduced the number of capital offences to just four, and there was a gradual move towards having a process of criminal appeal, so that in 1907 a court with that role was created.

The assizes continued until 1971, when they were superseded by Crown Courts. Obviously, most of the research done by family

---

COURTS OF LAW

SUPERIOR COURTS

<u>Supreme Court</u>

<u>Court of Appeal</u>

Civil Division	Criminal Division
(earlier Crown Cases Reserved)	1966 – after 1907 Act
High Court (after 1875)	**Crown Court**
Queen's Bench/Chancery/Family	(after 1972 – replacing assizes)

historians will be concerned with the actions and procedures in courts up to that time, and so in most cases assizes, magistrates' courts and county courts will be the ones most commonly used.

The court structure up until the establishment of Crown Courts in 1971 needs to be clear at the beginning of research; this was the procedure from the medieval period to recent times: the courts dealing with more serious affairs were (and still are) called superior courts, as summarised opposite.

The inferior courts, those dealing with the 'bread and butter' business of the legal system, were widely reported in the press and their records are diverse and wide-ranging, being found in the local and regional archives. The summary below shows their work and structure.

These courts from the summaries above need a brief explanation:

Coroners' courts: The first hearing for responses to deaths, suspicious or otherwise. These were often held in public houses.

Courts martial: A military court, where your criminal ancestor may have had his case heard, rather than in a criminal court.

Church courts: These have various names and have unusual jurisdiction, such as the Court of Arches, whose records are at Lambeth Palace. But church Consistory Courts would often sit in cathedrals and hear cases within the bishop's jurisdiction.

County Courts: The modern county courts were created by the County Courts Act of 1846, and there are 220, run by circuit judges. Procedure is in line with the County Court rules of 1936, and by the County Courts Act of 1959, their jurisdiction is either general –

INFERIOR COURTS

County Courts	Magistrates' Courts		Quarter Sessions	
Equity/probate/bankruptcy Criminal	Civil	Criminal	Civil	
	Husband & wife Bastardy	Summary offences juvenile	licensing	general

making it fall in line with the high courts – or special, which means that it worked in relation to the operation of statutes governing civil matters.

Where to find the main court records

Quarter Sessions Records: At your local County Record Office. Check the website of the archive first (put A2A into an internet search), then visit and use the index: this is extremely useful, summarising the material in the holdings.

Assize records: See TNA key for Criminal Trials 1559–1971 and Assizes, Welsh, 1831–1971. Click on 'assize records' at TNA website.

Old Bailey Sessions papers: For 1674–1913 they are searchable online. See www.oldbaileyonline.org

The Old Bailey is the Central Criminal Court in London. Today it is the Crown Court for the City of London, but the assize system did not apply to London, so offenders were held in Newgate prison and their cases were heard at eight annual sessions. Until 1539 there was no permanent courthouse, and the Court of Aldermen decided on the establishment of the Old Bailey as the court for the City. This new session house had jurisdiction over London, Middlesex and parts of other counties.

King's Bench (the highest criminal court): See TNA reference at KB2 for 1682–1985.

Police Courts: The quickest search is to use *The Times* Digital Archive and enter the name and date.

Chapter One
UNDERSTANDING THE LEGAL PROFESSIONS

The origins of the English legal system

To understand the nature of the development and definition of various legal professionals, it is necessary to explain the origins of the English law and how the courts developed. Before the courts acquired titles and identities, indicating their special concerns, the common law of England had steadily been created over the centuries, assimilating laws from customs and from the social fabric. Often defined as the 'common sense' precepts from unwritten law, it stands opposite in its nature and tradition from the specific courts developed in the Middle Ages, the idea of equity, which was codified by the Court of Chancery, and also from statute law – that law made by parliament.

Therefore, when the Norman Conquest of 1066 led to the centralisation of the regal power and administration, special courts began to be created. The *Aula Regis*, for instance, was the King's Court, or King's Hall was the new centre of the legal justice system. It led to the *Curia Regis* – the later form of the King's Court, which was the first stage towards the system of eyres and later assizes: varieties of courts 'on the move' across the King's realm.

The *Curia Regis* became an institution from which other courts were created: the Court of Common Pleas was an early one, at first being the only superior court dealing with ordinary civil actions, being controlled by five judges and the Lord Chief Justice. The *Common Bench* was the term for this sitting.

In family research, it is important to grasp the basis from which the later structures came.

MISS LETITIA WALKINGTON,
Ireland.

MISS FLORENCE CRONISE,
U.S.A.

MADAME E. KEMPIN-SPYRI,
Switzerland.

MRS. ELLENA KNOWLESS HASKELL,
U.S.A.

FRÄULEIN ANITA AUGSPURG,
Germany.

MRS. SHORTRIDGE FOLTZ,
U.S.A.

MISS CORNELIA SORABJI,
India.

MISS MARY GREENE,
U.S.A.

Some early women lawyers in 1890. The Graphic

Examples of early lawyers

In 1200, Stephen Boncretien was appointed as an attorney. After that he was given regular work, and was particularly active in the years between 1219 and 1223. He was a court clerk, appointed for litigation at the Common Bench, and his name appears on the plea rolls – the records for those suits. This was a sign that law as a profession, rather than as something that a literate man would dabble in when required, was emerging. In previous centuries, the ecclesiastical courts had naturally had their own staff in legal work, but for lay people in civil and in criminal courts, the practice had been for the plaintiff to take a friend or adviser to help in a court.

In the first years of the reign of Henry III (c.1216–1244), the serjeants of the Common Bench begin to be recorded. These were learned in the law, and they spoke for litigants; most people at Westminster started to use these serjeants. But more generally it seems that the kings throughout the thirteenth century gave legal work to amateurs who had a solid classical education. As Alan Harding has written, 'The lawyers of England, by this time, the thirteenth century, are worldly men . . . but they are in their way learned, cultivated men, linguists, logicians, tenacious disputants, true lovers of the nice case and the moot point.'

Judges began as councillors to the sovereigns; the King's Bench needed justices (and the King at times) to sit, and so this became a central source of the judiciary. Common law courts had so-called barons and chief barons to preside. But judges emerged as men who had a special training and an example of this would be Ralph of Hengham, who was first a judge's clerk, then a justice in the eyre (circuit hearing) and finally became a judge in Common Pleas by 1274. By the last decades of the fourteenth century there was an increasing demand for occupations in the law of a lesser degree to that of judge; working with them, a body of experienced attorneys developed across the land in various provinces.

The Middle Ages also saw the emergence of that standardisation of the vocabulary of law: there was 'law French' which made the legal profession more exclusive. A specific argot in a profession is part of its identity of course. More and more, writs and pleadings, the stuff of everyday law, was in the hands of the attorneys.

We have a sharp insight into the medieval lawyer from a very unusual source in *The Paston Letters*. These cover three generations of the Paston family of Norfolk, through the reigns of Henry VI, Edward IV and Richard III, so the lives of various people in the legal professions come alive there. William Paston, born in 1378, became a judge in 1429, having been a serjeant-at-law by 1421. He had also been a steward of the Duke of Norfolk. His son, John, born in 1421, went to the Inner Temple and was a knight of the shire. A relative, Elisabeth Clere, wrote to John to ask for legal advice and to ask him to consult another lawyer, writing:

> Cousin, I let you weet that Scrope hath been in this country to see my cousin your sister, and he hath spoken with my cousin your mother [cousin meant 'relative' at that time]. And she desireth him that he should show you the indentures made between the knight that hath his daughter and him: whether that Scrope, if he were married and fortuned to have children, if the children should inherit his land or his daughter the which is married . . .

We do not know the outcome, but it appears to have been a complex case, and the essential fact is that they are 'keeping it in the family' – this piece of legal business.

The coroner ('crowner')

The office of coroner dates back in some form or other to pre-Norman times, and there are mentions of coroners c.900, but it was in 1194 that the profession became something like today's coroner. He was a very important law officer, as he had duties relating to officiating at inquests and also, as he collected what were known as *deodands*, he was helpful in gathering income for the king. This is because the word deodand refers to the payment or forfeiture of belongings (chattels) to the sovereign after a death in some circumstances. They were abolished in 1846.

There had initially been opposition to coroners, but they had been becoming more necessary to the justice system throughout the reign of Henry II. This partly relates to the office of sheriff (*shire-reeve*) and sheriffs at the time of Henry II and Richard I were notorious for corruption: they were the most powerful officers of the law in their county. In 1170 there was an inquiry into the sheriffs and their practices; they were held back for the time being, many being deprived of office. But while Richard I was away from England, legal power was in the hands of his *justiciar*, his representative in the royal courts. The justiciar at this time, Hubert Walter, made the coroner a key member of staff in the campaign to raise money – hence the deodands.

After 1836 the coroner became very important with reference to certification: the Births and Deaths Act of that year made it compulsory either for a coroner's order or a registrar's certificate to be produced before a body could be buried. Then the Coroners Act of 1887 stated the duties of the coroner in more modern terms, abolishing some medieval elements of the work such as investigating shipwrecks; it also abolished the property qualification for the post. The kinds of people who generally applied for the post were from the middle classes, such as doctors and administrators.

Notaries and attorneys

The foundation of the legal profession at this early time in the development of law was the lay attorney. In the twelfth century a figure known as a *responsalis* appeared: the purpose of this position was to be a friend who saw to the process of law. Then, in the next century, the attorney was created. It has been suggested that it may have been the monks who first took these roles, as they were educated, and they could represent lay persons. In a court, the lay person's name would be called and the attorney would reply for him; the plaintiff's attorney would make sure that the case was called. Edward I spelled out the education required for these new professionals: in 1292 he ordered that 'The Chief Justice shall provide a certain number from every county of the better, worthier and more promising students . . . so chosen that they should follow the court and take part in its business, and no others.'

The word 'notary' goes back a very long way and *notarius* was used in classical times.

Basically, the need to convey a charter arose, and the notaries public came into being; contracts and conveyances developed in particular forms, and the writ-charter was made, authenticated by a seal. But, as has often been noted, seals could be forged, so there developed a need for trusted professionals to be involved. Contracts and conveyances as a consequence went to a law court, and by c.1250 a considerable amount of business was taking place and so there are substantial records. Official enrolments of private charters were allowed in the twelfth century and also in commerce, there was another development, of local authorities being made to create and record recognisances.

To sum up, the notary would find that all this business could come his way.

By the end of the thirteenth century the training of lawyers began to be more important in the minds of the senior legal officials. There are references to 'apprentices of the Common Bench' and it is clear that there were special areas in courts at this time at which these apprentices sat to listen and learn. In a case in 1302 the justice, Hengham, was recorded as having explained a legal rule for the benefit of the apprentices. There was also the production of court reports, which began to be produced around 1320; court reporters were by that time writing accounts of trials in such a way that students would be able to comprehend the often abstruse basis of the process.

Scholars have also found detailed notes within the texts of reports, so it seems fairly certain that there were teachers of law and that the reports were a fundamental teaching aid for them in class. There would also have been the formal disputes, affairs in which students would learn the elements of advocacy. These were known as *questiones disputate* and accounts of them have been discovered in several manuscripts from the fourteenth century. Even today, in universities where law is taught, there are similar teaching methods in use.

In the early fourteenth century, one lawyer had the following in his library: statutes of Edward I and II; Bracton and Britton (two law treatises); lawyer Hengham Magnum and Parvum on the nature of pleading; a register of writs; treatises on quashing writs, the duties of justice, and on Pleas of the Crown. He also had Year Books. These were records of trials but they did not record outcomes; it is generally thought that the Year Books were purposely made simply to record the findings, not the results. They formed the only valid records of courts. Law reporting was not considered to be right, and on one occasion a notary was found making notes and a serjeant called Stonor said to Chief Justice Bereford, 'Sir, see here a notary who, by the plaintiff's procurement, has come privily to watch this law-making to our prejudice and in deceit of the court.' The notary was charged. RG Hamilton has written that the Year Books were probably compiled to teach the art of pleading. He notes:

> Students had to learn the 30 different writs and their applications; the Year Books certainly showed them in practice. Occasionally the Year Book reporter gave his own opinion. There was a case in 1313 about pasture rights in Abingdon. At the close of the pleadings, it was decided that the ultimate question for the jury was for how long the Abbot and his predecessors had enjoyed the pasture rights. 'And I am of the opinion,' says the Year Book compiler, ' . . . that was not the issue which should have been taken.' (RG Hamilton: see the bibliography.)

The legal profession, by 1300, was obviously well established. In 1292 there was an ordinance attempting to limit the number of professional attorneys, so there must have been problems in the ranks of these people – probably some kind of corruption or malpractice. A cynical view would aver that where there is corruption there is considerable power, and in any profession, that is inextricably linked to trust. The important point in this context is that by around 1300 there was no necessity for a man to be a cleric in order to be called to the Bar to practise law. We may often find names of practitioners in a variety of legal documents, so research for ancestors before the Tudor period in particular, may be found in such places as fine rolls, for instance, where this kind of entry may be found:

> Nov. 9 Westminster: Commitment to Laurence de Allerthor, Clerk, one of the barons of the Exchequer – by mainprise of John Skylling in the County of Wilts . . .
> Nov. 18 Westminster: Grant to John de Scardeburgh, clerk of the Chancery of the keeping of all the lands late of John de Warwick . . .

The names of the lawyers are there, and many of these fine rolls have been printed by HMSO and so there are indexes to the volumes. It is not entirely a fruitless task to try to locate ancestors who may have been notaries in the medieval period. For instance, there was a return of the names of notaries in the diocese of London sent by the Bishop of London to the Archbishop of Canterbury in 1402; this lists twenty men working in that capacity, and some have definitions of their duties attached to their names, such as Johannes Perche *curia cantuariensis registrarius* (the registrar for the Cambridge court).

The Assizes

It is a great help to the family history researcher to know the outline history and nature of the assize courts, so a summary of them and their beginnings is necessary here. The word comes from the Latin *assideo* – to sit together. Itinerant justices were appointed after the Assize of Clarendon in 1166 and then again in 1196 at the Council of Northampton.

After Magna Carta (1215) two courts were created which were to be in the regions: they were the assize of *novel disseisin* and the assize of *mort d'ancestor*. The former was a hearing regarding claims to a land which had been lost by a previous owner. The latter court was to have proceedings to regain land previously owned in a family and which had been taken unjustly. Justices had to travel into the provinces to be present at these courts, and so the assizes developed. As time passed, a regular number of circuits was established and two justices would travel each circuit, one judge for civil matters and the other for criminal. In Magna Carta, Section 18 states:

Land disputes shall be taken only in their proper counties and in this manner; we, or if we be absent from the realm our chief justiciar shall send two justiciars through each county four times a year and they together with four knights . . . shall hold the said assize . . .

These later circuits of the assizes were printed in *The Gentleman's Magazine* and in almanacs. The main actions they performed were *oyez and terminer* – to try serious cases such as treason and murder (and other felonies) and gaol delivery, which meant that they had to try every person who had been languishing behind bars since the last assize.

Assizes were held twice a year, in Lent and Summer; the circuits dealt with all English counties except Cheshire, Durham, Lancashire and Middlesex.

Below is an extract from the circuits information from *The Gentleman's Magazine* in 1806.

Crown courts arrived in 1971 and so the assizes were abolished. In 1972, a former judge, Basil Neild, published *Farewell to the Assizes*, in which he described every circuit and gave an account of the lawyers he had worked with. There he gives a full account of the history and nature of the assizes. Neild sat at every one of the sixty-one assize towns in England and Wales. Anyone wanting a full account of the assize system will find no better explanation than Neild's book.

For civil courts, a summary of what topics the civil courts have dealt

CIRCUITS OF THE JUDGES					
SPRING	Norfolk	Midland	Home	Western	Oxford
Northern					
CIRCUIT					
March 1	L Ellenborough	L C Justice	L C Baron	B Thomson	J Lawrence J
Rooke					
Aylesbury	J. Grose	B. Graham	J. Heath	J Le Blanc	B Sutton J
Chambre					
March 3		**North'ton**			**Reading**
March 4				**Winchester**	

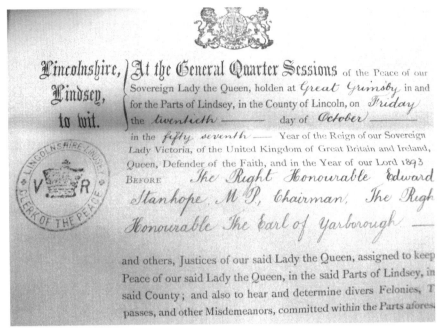

Lincolnshire, **At the General Quarter Sessions** of the Peace of our
Lindsey, Sovereign Lady the Queen, holden at *Great Grimsby* in and
to wit. for the Parts of Lindsey, in the County of Lincoln, on *Friday*
the *twentieth* — day of *October* —
in the *fifty seventh* — Year of the Reign of our Sovereign
Lady Victoria, of the United Kingdom of Great Britain and Ireland,
Queen, Defender of the Faith, and in the Year of our Lord 1893
BEFORE *The Right Honourable Edward*
Stanhope M.P, Chairman, The Righ
Honourable The Earl of Yarborough —

and others, Justices of our said Lady the Queen, assigned to keep
Peace of our said Lady the Queen, in the said Parts of Lindsey, in
said County; and also to hear and determine divers Felonies, T
passes, and other Misdemeanors, committed within the Parts afores

Edward Stanhope becomes Keeper of the Peace, 1894. Lincolnshire Archives

with since the important Judicature Act of 1875, makes the research process easier. The High Court deals with family, chancery and Queen's Bench matters today, and since 1875, each is housed in a 'division':

Family Division: this deals with divorce and child welfare, and with the administration of wills. Most divorce cases are heard in the county courts.

Chancery Division: this deals with disputes concerning wills, settlements and trusts, land law, and law relating to intellectual property such as copyright disputes. It also took over bankruptcy cases after 1875.

Queen's Bench Division: this is mainly concerned with cases relating to contracts, torts or land. A *tort* is a civil wrong, as opposed to a criminal offence. An example would be the notion of negligence, which may be a tort (and so tried in a civil court) or a criminal offence and so heard in a criminal court.

Chapter Two
THE COMMUNITY OF LAWYERS

The Bar

The serjeants, discussed in the previous chapter, became linked with the wearing of the *coif*, after a key event in 1207. That was the date on which arose the problem of the clergy doing law work in courts which were outside the ecclesiastical domain, and so they were forbidden to act as pleaders in temporal courts. Some priests still carried on with the work and wore a coif to cover their tonsure; the barrister's wig may well have had its origins in this development.

As the lawyers became professionalised, and as they were mostly congregated around London, there arose the need for their accommodation and their training. For this, the inns of court began to be established. Land formerly in the possession of the earls of Lincoln and the Knights Templar, and from the Lords de Grey of Wilton, was acquired and so there emerged Lincoln's Inn, the Temple and Gray's Inn. Later the inns of chancery were added to these inns of court. Wealthy men and the sons of the aristocrats were housed and trained at the inns of court, whereas the inns of chancery were for sons of merchants, called *apprenticii*. An anonymous old rhyme also suggested this demarcation:

> *The Inner for the rich man;*
> *The Middle for the poor;*
> *Lincoln's Inn for the gentleman,*
> *And Gray's Inn for the poor.*

This community of lawyers was, in effect, a university. Of these inns, in the time of Elizabeth I, nine were within the liberties of the

AGE 2. [Miniature.

From a] AGE 19. [Painting.

AGE 16. R. TAYLOR & C°
From a Water-Colour
by Mrs. Hawkins.

AGE 50. [Drawing.

AGE 70. From a Photo. by] [Whitlock, Birmingham.

LORD COLERIDGE.

BORN 1821.

HE RIGHT HON. JOHN DUKE COLERIDGE, Lord Chief Justice of England, was born at Heath's Court, Ottery Mary, and educated at Eton (at which time our second portrait presents him), and at Balliol College, Oxford, where he was an undergraduate at nineteen, the age of our third portrait. He was called to the bar in 1846, and after a brilliant career at fifty, the age of our fourth portrait, made Attorney-General. Two years later was raised to the peerage by the title of Baron Coleridge, of Ottery St. Mary. In 1880 he was made Lord Chief Justice of England, and is, as need hardly here be added, one of the most brilliant ornaments of the British bench, which consists, now as ever, of some of the finest intellects and characters of their generation.

Celebrated lawyers. Author's collection

city (the areas within the borough) and five were outside this. In 1615, the writer Sir George Buc referred to the Inn of Chancery as 'the third university of England'. The Four Inns became the Inner Temple, Middle Temple, Lincoln's Inn and Gray's Inn. Three classes of members were established: the benchers, senior lawyers and judges – being the governors of each inn; the barristers who are called by the benchers, and the students. Writing in 1919, JA Strahan assessed the changes which had happened in the course of the previous century:

> Lincoln's Inn chambers were used almost entirely as business places for practising barristers and for solicitors who lived elsewhere. But the higher floors of the houses in the Temple were then filled by the younger barristers and the older students of the two Inns. Things have changed since that time. The two inns' younger members have now, like so many of our brave soldiers, 'gone West' but in a different and less noble way. (*The Bench and Bar of England*)

There were radical changes made in the Bar throughout the nineteenth century. At the heart of this was the Bar Council. From the seventeenth century the right to practise as an advocate in the Royal Courts was restricted to members of the Inns, and so the Bar became the regulating body. Judges have been responsible for the orderly functioning of the Bar since the fourteenth century; then in 1894 the General Council of the Bar was formed to supervise and regulate professional behaviour. There was a general meeting of the Bar in July 1894 under the presidency of the Attorney-General, and with the brief that 'It is expedient and necessary that the representative organisation of the Bar should be improved.' Regulations were drawn up and a board selected to represent the legal profession.

We can see the respective individuality of the Inns and of the Bar a year later when the General Bar Council chose a team to meet with representatives of the Inns of Court to discuss the amount of financial contributions made by the Inns to the Bar Council each year. At the end of the meeting, it was resolved that, as *The Times* reported: '. . . but in making such grant the Inns of Court do not recognize that the Bar

The close of a tedious trial. Author's collection

Council has any right to exercise any of the jurisdiction, powers or privileges of the Inns of Court.'

The Bar Council was always looking to improve standards and regulation in those years of change, and in 1901 issues were reported and debated in the press around professional matters such as 'May a counsel accept in London a brief from a solicitor who has not a London certificate without the intervention of a London agent? May a barrister practise while he is acting as public analyst under the Sale of Food and Drugs Act?' (*The Times*, April 4, 1901).

When there were public scandals involving barristers, there was usually a commotion and action was taken. In 1836, for instance, a barrister called Fitzroy Kelly was suspected of corruption at a parliamentary election in Ipswich. Where the lawyers met to drink together as the assize circuit progressed, the topic was discussed; the closely-guarded and friendly establishment of the circuit Mess – this one in the Norfolk Circuit – was the heart of the argument, as Kelly wished to introduce a new man into the fraternity, with Kelly head-to-head with a man called Andrews. The latter and his friends formed a new group called a 'club' and by having a majority vote, they excluded the new man. This scandal revealed a great deal about the legal fraternity around the Bar at the time, and it shows how the circuit members regulated behaviour in their own ways.

The Temple and some of the Benchers were the subject of a famous essay by the writer Charles Lamb, and in his essay, *The Old Benchers of the Inner Temple,* he describes the location of this prestigious Inn:

> I was born, and passed the first seven years of my life, in the Temple, its church, its halls, its gardens, its fountains, its river . . . Indeed it is the most elegant spot in the metropolis. What a transition for a countryman visiting London for the first time – the passing from the crowded Strand or Fleet Street, by unexpected avenues, into its magnificent ample squares, its classic green recesses!

Today, the place is exactly the same as Lamb saw it.

The Law Society itself had its origins in the modern period in a group called The Society of Gentlemen Practisers. The early records were thought to have been lost but in a journal called *T. P.'s Weekly* in 1870 an answer to a question about records had this information:

> A few years ago an old box in the Law Society's vaults on being opened was found to contain the Minute Book and other manuscripts relating to the Society of Gentlemen Practisers. These were classified and arranged under the direction of the Law Society and a selection of them, with an introduction by Dr Edwin Freshfield, has been published under the title The Records of the Society of Gentlemen Practisers in the Courts of Law and Equity called the Law Society, 1739 to 1810. For those who find an interest in the everyday life of the lawyers of a bygone generation this volume will provide a veritable storehouse of delight . . .

For the family historian, these matters are important to understand, as all barrister and solicitor ancestors would have been aware of the issues, and some would have been affected by them, of course.

Coming up to date, it should be noted that in 1974, the Bar Council and the governing body of the Inns of Court combined to form the Senate of the Inns of Court and the Bar. Then, in 1990, a council of the Inns of Court was created again, maintaining the old independence.

If we ask what barristers do and what is at the heart of the profession, no better explanation may be given than that by Dr Johnson, after he responded to a statement by Sir William Forbes, who thought that an honest lawyer should never undertake a cause which he was not satisfied was a just one. Johnson responded:

> Sir, a lawyer has no business with the justice or injustice of the cause which he undertakes, unless his client asks his opinion, and then he is bound to give it honestly. The justice or injustice of the cause is to be decided by the judge. Consider Sir, what is the purpose of the courts of justice? It is that every man may have his cause fairly tried, by men appointed to try causes. (*Tour to the Hebrides*, by James Boswell.)

Specialisation and local history sources

The family historian needs to know something about the nature of the particular aspect of law the ancestor worked in. The foregoing background has been included to provide a foundation for this understanding.

With all this diversity and complexity in the historical development of the legal profession, it becomes clear that your ancestor most certainly specialised in one area of legal work and in one branch of the profession. In the memoirs of lawyers there are plenty of accounts and explanations of this specialisation. Perhaps one of the best-known is the case of John Mortimer, the writer. In his essay, *Law and Justice* Mortimer explains the work he did in the Probate, Divorce and Admiralty Division. As he says there, 'Probate cases were the ones in which ruthless relatives fought tooth and nail for the furniture.' His essay focuses mainly on divorce at the time (the 1940s) and it typifies the kind of literature needed in family history research, because the text books and historical works will not give you the real feel of the everyday legal work your ancestor did.

Mortimer explains that 'Matrimonial law had come down from the ecclesiastical courts, through the years when women couldn't own property or divorce their husbands for cruelty . . . when I started just after the war a husband could still get damages from his wife's lover. This entailed an argument in court about her value in hard cash.' Fortunately, for present purposes, there has been a vast library of legal memoirs through the centuries (discussed in chapter 7) and writers have been only too pleased to explain their cases. But of course this applies only to high-profile people such as barristers, serjeants-at-law and judges. What about the solicitors?

One of the best ways to enquire into the everyday work of solicitors, coroners, justices' clerks and so on is to look into local history. For instance, the Hedon & District Local History Society has recently included in its newsletter a feature on 'Robert Carrick, Solicitor and mayor of Hedon'. As the article states, the practice was a family one, and the writer points out that 'most of the property in Holderness has at one time or another passed through the hands of Mr Carrick'. There is more on this in chapter 5.

Local history publications often present insights into the lives of lawyers and others. The point to make here is that any enquiry into a solicitor's collections will immediately lead the researcher into areas of social life of all kinds: this shows how easy it is to fill out the picture of the fuller, wider life in the community of the solicitor or other legal professional. For example, solicitors dealt with apprenticeship indentures and with beer house licensing; those subjects open up all kinds of social issues very much of their time.

A typical example of this is an article by Paul Jennings in *The Local Historian* in which he looks at the Licensing Act of 1904. In the course of that essay it becomes clear that licensing in that context had given the solicitors plenty of work. He notes that in the nineteenth century, before that Act, 'The result was a body of law of great and (with the passage of time and ever more legislation) growing complexity. Despite consolidating statutes . . . with respect to drunkenness it remained so. To it must be added a huge mass of excise measures resulting in, as Lord Chief Justice Cockburn described it, "a labyrinth of chaotic legislation".' This is a template example of how understanding the contemporary factors around the worker in the legal machine is a necessary foundation for research.

Some early publications

It is useful for the family historian to know something about some accounts of the legal profession as the duties were being fashioned, and also to be aware of the formative works which every lawyer would have known.

In terms of the professional manuals, a typical example is that by Sir John Doderidge, Knight, 'one of the justices of the King's Bench' and published in 1631, simply called *The English Lawyer*. The title page states that it is concerned with 'expressing the best qualities requisite in the student, practiser, judges and fathers of the laws of the land'. In explaining the desired qualities of a judge, for instance, Doderidge writes that he should be religious, a man of courage, a man of integrity, a man able to 'discern circumstances' and he ought to be learned.

Commentaries on the Laws of England (1765–1769), by Sir William Blackstone, began as a course of lectures the great jurist gave at Oxford. He was explaining the complexities of the law to laymen and in writing the book he created the first real survey of English law. He dealt with the fundamental common law and also provided, as the great historian, JH Baker has written, 'the first textbook of a new legal era'.

The two most outstanding writers on law in the sixteenth and seventeenth centuries were Sir Matthew Hale and Sir Edward Coke. Coke wrote *The Institutes of the Laws of England* at the age of 64 but the work was not in print until 1628. He had produced a handbook, a work invaluable to young men entering the law. Parts of the great work were suppressed after his death in 1634. That has to be some kind of tribute to the achievement. On the other hand, Hale, who was Chief Justice on the King's Bench, had a massive influence on the nature and conceptual framework of English criminal law. His classic works were published after his death: *History of the Common Law* in 1713 and *The History of the Pleas of the Crown* in 1736.

THE
ENGLISH
LAWYER.

DESCRIBING

A Method for the managing of the
Lawes of this Land.

And expreſſing the beſt qualities requiſite in the

⎧ *Student*
⎨ *Practizer* ⎬ of the ſame.
⎩ *Judges* and *Fathers* ⎭

Written by the Reverend and Learned Sir IOHN
DODERIDGE Knight, one of the Iuſtices
of the Kings Bench, lately deceaſed.

L O N D O N,
Printed by the Aſſignes of I. MORE Eſq.
M DC XXXI.

Title page of The English Lawyer, *1631. Author's collection*

As well as these great works, there were everyday functional manuals prepared for justices, coroners and others. These will be explained when each profession is discussed later. These became so influential that they were referred to simply by name, such as 'Jervis' or 'Archbold' and this would be part of the common vocabulary of the community of legal professionals.

Case Study: Staple Inn

In 2005, I acquired a copy of *Staple Inn and its Story* by T Cato Worsfold, published in 1913. It was clearly the author's own copy and within the covers I discovered poems and annotations made by Worsfold. Everywhere in those careful manuscript notes there is evidence of the writer's deep love of his alma mater. It was a convivial community, a truly professional place of learning as well as of fraternity. For the family historian, it has great value, as Worsfold lists 'principals and worthies' of the Inn going back to 1716. This was drawn from the Roll of Admissions; the names were all principals and had their own armorial bearings. There are forty names listed. Worsfold also provides biographical sketches of most of these people, so we have an anecdotal history of one of the Inns.

What is more useful to family historians is that Worsfold's life and career illustrates an important point in researching lawyers' lives: move laterally into the social circle of the person as well as chronologically. In other words, Worsfold was not only chairman of Eastwoods Ltd, he was the legal advisor to the Royal Society of Literature and the Royal Historical Society; he also attended Guildhall meetings, wrote on classical studies, and generally appears to have been a speaker and a man who was drawn to convivial company among his peers. Many legal professionals will have had similar lifestyles. A cursory search in *The Times* Digital Archives gave a profile of Mr Worsfold, and certainly a similar search in local and regional newspapers should bring something similar on the ancestor's life.

Staple Inn itself has its origins in the link with the 'staple' towns, that is those which dealt in staple produce: lead, leather, wool and so on. T Cato Worsfold also explains another origin of the word: ' . . . it is an interesting fact that the Old English word Stapel signified a heap, hence a spot where objects of merchandise were collected for purpose of sale and barter, from which it is easy to see that the articles forming the 'stapel' became, in the expansion and progress of trade, known by that name themselves . . . '

The Inn was an Inn of Chancery as far back as the early years of the fifteenth century, in the reign of Henry V. As part of the centres of learning which formed all the Inns, the training done there would have included what are known as 'moots'. These are formal discussions on legal topics, put forward by the students, carried out in the presence of a bencher and two barristers who act as judges. Moot days were organised for Tuesdays and Thursdays in the reign of Charles II for instance; there were also grand moots, occasions held as events preliminary to someone being called to the Bar.

Staple Inn, on the south side of High Holborn, is today the London office of the Institute of Actuaries. Despite damage done during the Blitz, it has survived in part and has been restored. But as an inn for lawyers, it ended its days in 1884, being sold to a firm of auctioneers.

It may be seen from this that the Inns were, and are, the centres of education and professional regulation, as well as fraternities, for lawyers.

Chapter Three
THE JUDGES AND THE COURTS

Judges: an historical survey

In September 2009, it was announced that judges were to be 'put on trial' to test their courtroom skills. *The Times* reported that judges would have to 'go back to school' under a radical new training programme.

From April 2010, there will be fifteen new courses on offer for full-time judges. The programme will mean that every judge will have to have at least a four-day residential course every year in order to be refreshed, up-dated and tested. Lord Justice Maurice Kay and Judge John Phillips will be in charge of matters. The Lord Chief Justice told the press: 'Judicial work is essentially an isolated activity and one judge very rarely sees how another judge sets about his or her work . . . judicial education gives judges an opportunity . . . to discuss and share good practice . . . '

Such a development would have been looked upon as absurd and outrageous by many of the powerful judges of the past, whose memoirs are a testimony to their extremely potent and high-status situation. After all, in criminal trials up and down the land, until 1964 judges donned the black cap and passed the sentence of death on prisoners in the dock. The general public perception of judges, as we see them in popular culture, is of men in robes and wigs with incredible power over the wretched prisoner in the dock. But their origins lie in their role as advisers to the King, and from there they linked with the justices of the King's Bench. The three Common Law courts came from this, and so it became general practice for three judges to sit in each of the three courts: in Chancery, King's Bench and the High Court of Justice.

Lord Russell, one of the celebrities of the judiciary. Strand Magazine

We can understand the power and status of the judge if we look at the operation of what was called Crown Cases Reserved. These records are in print (published by a company called Cox – see bibliography) and they provide a chronicle of a very special court. If, in a trial at assizes, a judge considered that there was a point of law which should be resolved by a group of his peers, then the Crown Cases

The London Guildhall, setting for the court of aldermen. The author

Reserved assembly of judges was gathered, for a decision. These were recorded in volumes, by circuit (following the assizes).

For example, in 1883 a certain Jane Clark was indicted at Durham Assizes for a 'nuisance' which was in this case 'exposing the body of a child in a public highway'. This was a Common Law misdemeanour, and Judge Denman told the jury, 'I am not at all sure that this case is free from doubt in point of law.' Denman finally announced that he had consulted his fellow judges and he arrived at the decision that Jane had indeed committed an offence under the Common Law. She was sentenced to six months in prison.

Specific terms for certain varieties of judge will occur in research. A

Judge's lodgings, Lincoln. The author

typical example is the *Recorder*. In the years before 1971 when Crown Courts were created, a recorder was a barrister who would act as a justice of the peace. In 1850, for instance, the office of Recorder of London was vacant after the death of the Hon CE Law. This was in the City of London and so the office was decided by the aldermen. Four barristers were considered for this eminent post and three refused the offer. Eventually Mr JA Stuart Wortley accepted. In the report in *The Times*, the duties of the office were listed at that time, the main ones being:

- To advise the Court of Lord Mayor and aldermen for their better direction in administering law and justice
- To attend and advise the Lord Mayor and aldermen of Hustings and in the Mayor's court for equity as well as for common law
- Being by charter a justice of the peace for London . . . . To attend and assist the Lord Mayor of this City

(*The Times*, 21.9.1850)

Judges in the Court Reports

Judges were named and their actions briefly reported in the press. In the 1850s, Charles Dickens's *Household Narrative*, as noted earlier, provided summary reports under 'Law and Crime' and a glance at the 1854 collected volumes has reports from these courts: Marlborough Street Police Court; a coroner's inquest at Hunslet in Leeds, and the Court of Queen's Bench sitting in Dublin. Criminal ancestors were present at all these locations, with crimes ranging from 'stealing a bit of velvet ribbon' to a case of 'wilful murder against Joseph Baines' who was charged with killing his wife. Such is the proliferation of courts and trials in British history and the family historian needs to find a way through this labyrinth.

In the fuller reports given in such publications as *The Gentleman's Magazine* and *The Annual Register*, judges' actions and words may be more detailed in the summary of the cases.

Judges in the County Courts

These were established by the County Courts Act of 1846, and the purpose of these courts was mainly to 'make . . . expedient to alter and regulate the manner and proceed in the said courts for the recovery of small debts and demands'. Section IX of that Act defines the appointment of judges:

> And be it enacted, that the Lord Chancellor shall appoint as many fit persons as are needed to be judges of the County Court under this Act, each of whom shall be a barrister-at-law who shall be of seven years standing, or who shall have practised as a barrister and Special Pleader for at least seven years.

For records of judges in their county court roles, TNA has material at CAB 24/193 and at CAB/46, relating to salaries. The County Court Acts of 1846, 1888 and 1903 had repercussions on the status and work of the County Court judges, and the relevant materials are under miscellaneous sources from the records of the Cabinet Office.

Lord Eldon, Lord Chancellor of the Regency years. Author's collection

QUARTER-SESSIONS (1859)
IN THE SEVERAL COUNTIES OF ENGLAND AND WALES.

By the Act 1 Will. IV. c. 70, it is enacted that " in the year 1831, and afterwards, the justices of the peace in every county, riding, or division, for which Quarter-Sessions of the Peace by law ought to be held, shall hold their general Quarter-Sessions of the Peace in the first whole week after the 11th of October, in the first week after the 28th of December, in the first week after the 31st of March, and in the first week after the 24th of June." The following list has been computed according to this rule.

The Act 4 and 5 Will. IV. cap. 47, allows a discretionary power to the Justices of Peace as to the time of holding the Spring Quarter-Sessions, and empowers them to alter the day for holding the Sessions, so as not to be earlier than the 7th of March, nor later than the 22d of April.

BEDFORD—W. Jan. 5, April 6, June 29, Oct. 19.

BERKS—M. *Abingdon*, Jan. 3, June 27, *Reading*, April 4, Oct. 17.

BUCKS—*Aylesbury*, Tu. Jan. 4, April 5, June 28, Oct. 18.

CAMBRIDGE—*Cambridge* County, F. Jan. 7, April 8, July 1, Oct. 21.

CHESHIRE—M. *Chester*, same as *Berks*.

CORNWALL—*Bodmin*, Tu. same as *Bucks*. April 5 at *Truro*.

CUMBERLAND—Tu. as *Bucks*, Jan. and June at *Carlisle*, April & Oct. at *Cockermouth*.

DERBYSHIRE—April Sessions at *Chesterfield*, the others at *Derby*, Tu. same as *Bucks*.

DEVONSHIRE—*Exeter*, Tu. same as *Bucks*.

DORSETSHIRE—*Dorchester*, Tu. as *Bucks*.

DURHAM—M. same as *Berks*.

ELY, Isle of—W. as *Bedford*, at *Wisbeach*, Jan. and June, at *Ely*, April and Oct.

ESSEX—*Colchester* and *Harwich*, M. same as *Berks*. *Chelmsford*, Tu. as *Bucks*.

GLOUCESTERSHIRE—*Gloster*, Tu. as *Bucks*.

HAMPSHIRE—*Winchester*, Tu. as *Bucks*.

HEREFORDSHIRE—*Hereford*, M. as *Berks*.

HERTFORDSHIRE — *Hertford*, M. same as *Berks*. *St. Alban's*, the same week.

HUNTINGDONSHIRE—M. same as *Berks*.

KENT—*Canterbury*, Tu. Jan. 4, Fr. Apr. 8, Tu. June 28, Fr. Oct. 21. *Maidstone*, Th. Jan. 6, Tu. Apr. 5, Th. June 30, Tu. Oct. 18.

LANCASHIRE—*Lancaster*, Tu. same as *Bucks*. Adjournments are held at Preston, at Salford, and at Kirkdale.

LEICESTERSHIRE—*Leicester*, M. as *Berks*.

LINCOLNSHIRE—
Parts of Lindsey.
Kirton . . . . | Fr. Jan. 7, April 8, July 1, Oct. 21
Louth . . . . | Tu. ——, April 12, ——, Oct. 25
Spilsby . . . | Tu. Jan. 11, ——, July 5, ——
Bourn and *Boston*, M. as *Berks*; *Sleaford*, and *Spalding*, Th. Jan. 6, April 7, June 30, Oct. 20.

MIDDLESEX—General or adjourned Sessions are held at least twice a month at the Sessions House, *Clerkenwell*, usually on the alternate Tuesdays; and adjourned Sessions are also held at Westminster (Broad Sanctuary). The LONDON Sessions are held four times a year at the Guildhall. The *Tower Liberty* Sessions are held eight times a year at the Sessions House, Wellclose-square.

MONMOUTHSHIRE—*Usk*, M. as *Berks*.

NORFOLK — *Shire House*, *Norwich*, Tu. same as *Bucks*.

NORTHAMPTONSHIRE — *Northampton*, W. as *Bedford*. *Peterborough*, same days.

NORTHUMBERLAND — *Newcastle-on-Tyne*, W. Jan. 5, *Morpeth*, Apr. 6, *Hexham*, June 29, *Alnwick*, Oct. 19, *Berwick*, F. Oct. 21.

NOTTINGHAMSHIRE—
Nottingham, M. as *Berks*.
Newark, F. as *Cambridge*.
East Retford, M. after *Newark*.

OXFORDSHIRE—M. as *Berks*. *Banbury*, the preceding Saturday.

RUTLANDSHIRE—*Oakham*, W. as *Bedford*.

SHROPSHIRE — *Shrewsbury*, M. as *Berks*. For the Town, the Friday after.

SOMERSETSHIRE — Tu. *Taunton*, Jan. 4, June 28. *Wells*, April 5, Oct. 18.

STAFFORDSHIRE—*Stafford*, W. as *Bedford*.

SUFFOLK—*Beccles*, M. as *Berks*, *Woodbridge*, W. as *Bedford*, *Ipswich*, F. as *Cambridge*; and *Bury*, M. as Berks.

SURREY—*New Sessions House*, *Newington*, Tu. Jan. 4. *Reigate*, April 5. *Guildford*, June 28. *Kingston*, Oct. 18.

SUSSEX — Eastern Division: *Lewes*, M. same as *Berks*. Western Division: *Petworth*, Th. Jan. 6, and April 7. *Horsham*, June 30. *Chichester*, Oct. 20.

WARWICKSHIRE—*Warwick*, Tu. as *Bucks*.

WESTMINSTER—City, are generally held on the Thursday preceding the Quarter-Sessions for *Middlesex*.

WESTMORLAND—W. *Appleby*, Jan. and June, *Kendal*, April and Oct.

WILTSHIRE—Tu. *Devizes*, Jan. 4. *Salisbury*, April 5. *Warminster*, June 28. *Marlborough*, Oct. 18.

WORCESTERSHIRE—*Worcester*, M. same as *Berks*.

YORKSHIRE—EAST RIDING: *Beverley*, Tu. as *Bucks*. WEST RIDING: *Wakefield*, Tu. Jan. 4. *Sheffield*, F. Jan. 7. *Pontefract*, M. April 4. *Skipton*, M. June 27. *Bradford*, Tu. June 28. *Rotherham*, F. July 1. *Knaresborough*, M. Oct. 17. *Leeds*, Tu. Oct. 18. *Doncaster*, F. Oct. 21. NORTH RIDING: *Northallerton*, Tu. as *Bucks*.

——

The Quarter Sessions through NORTH and SOUTH WALES are held by the same rule as the foregoing, the magistrates determining the day of the week on which the Sessions shall commence.

It has been found necessary to omit the sessions for *Cities* and *Towns*, as they may be changed according to the will of the Recorder.

Quarter Sessions lists from the British Almanac, 1859. *Author's collection*

More information in assize reports

These were held from the thirteenth century until 1971. The system had its origins in which two judges would hold the sovereign's court twice a year. These tried criminal cases and civil. From 1550 records provide details of such offences as homicide, infanticide and major theft. Before 1733 assize records are in Latin and the main records are indictments (statements of charges); depositions (written evidences) and gaol books or minutes (lists of accused persons) and summaries of cases heard. If there are no assize records surviving, then there are sheriffs' assize vouchers, located at TNA E389 and also, for writs, the King's Bench records.

The Gentleman's Magazine published details of the assize circuits, such as this entry from the 1819 issue: 'Spring Circuits, 1819: Norfolk, Lord Chief Justice Abbott and baron Graham: Aylesbury, March 4, Bedford March 10, Huntingdon March 13, Thetford March 20, Bury St Edmunds March 26.'

Officials in the criminal justice system

It is also worthwhile to be reminded of the functions of various offices within the criminal justice system. The main ones are:

Coroner

Under the Normans, he was 'the keeper of the pleas of the crown' and so was a 'crowner'. The coroner sits at inquests and also used to define what *deodands* (payments to the crown) would be paid.

Justice of the Peace

An act of 1327 stated that a person had to be appointed in each county to be responsible for keeping the peace of the sovereign. The Justices of the Peace Act in 1361 defined them as justices, and they were usually powerful locals such as Lords of the Manor.

Lord Lieutenant

He was originally a military householder, but then, since the sixteenth century, he has been the representative of the sovereign in the county at the highest level. He was also responsible for keeping the county records, and was the person who organised militia and communal defence in emergency.

Parish Constable

At first he was appointed by the court leet of the manor – a court hearing all kinds of offences. He had to supervise watch and ward, the first real system of community vigilance, but he also had several other duties, including impounding stray animals and supervising beggars and vagrants.

Sheriff

This was originally a 'shire reeve' – the deputy of the crown. He was the main organiser of the courts before the justices appeared, and he ran the militia.

Civil Courts

In the English criminal justice system, civil courts – dealing with civil offences, not criminal ones – have been numerous and complex in their hierarchies. The system has always been founded on inferior and superior courts: the inferior courts included these civil courts:

- *County courts, covering Common Law, probate, equity, bankruptcy and so on. These are called Civil Bill Courts in Ireland*
- *Civil cases before magistrates*
- *Civil cases before the quarter sessions*
- *Civil cases before the coroner*
- *Administrative tribunals*

In the superior courts all matters relating to high court cases were heard, and these courts were (and still are except for assizes):

- *Court of Appeal*
- *High Court*
- *Crown Court*
- *Courts Martial Appeal Court*
- *Restrictive Practices Court*
- *Employment Appeal Tribunal*

In addition to this, any court dealing with important cases would be included, such as what were formerly the palatine courts of Lancaster and Durham.

In family history research for legal ancestors, the historian will have to access and understand these courts and know where the records are. Fortunately, the Law Reports over the centuries are helpful in this, if one knows the approximate dates during which the ancestor was in practice. These reports are in print and are found in a university library where law is taught. Mozley and Whiteley's *Law Dictionary* has listings of major law reports and the dates they cover, so for instance, there we have this kind of entry:

REPORTS	ABBREVIATIONS	DATE	COURT
England	All Eng.	1936 to present	All courts
Atkyns	Atk.	1736–1754	Chancery
Bunbury	Bunb	1713–1741	Exchequer

Chapter Four
THE MAGISTRACY

The Quarter Sessions

The Quarter Sessions courts were always the workhorse of the criminal justice system throughout British history. They began in 1361, and handled every kind of offence and local tribulation that came their way. They were the domain of the justices of the peace (magistrates) and met, as the name suggests, four times a year. Before the justices came concerns related to drunkenness, pub brawls, arguments over land, nuisances on the highway, problems with beggars, licensing of beer houses, provision of constables, maintenance of bridges and other affairs, the topics changing as the years passed and society had new laws and fresh social problems.

Matters were running smoothly through the years until an Act of 1831 which stipulated specific dates for the courts, so as not to interfere with the assizes (which dealt with felonies, more serious crime). This statute said: ' . . . Quarter Sessions for the peace by law ought to be held . . . in the first week after the 11th of October, in the first week after the 28th of December, in the first week after the 31st of March, and in the first week after the 24th of June.' From the early nineteenth century, details of the sessions were given in almanacs, sometimes locally but always in the *British Almanac*, published by the Society for the Diffusion of Useful Knowledge. This publication listed all the quarter sessions for the coming year, with dates and venues.

It was in the Tudor period that the justices really found their workload accelerating: a succession of legislative measures to deal with the increasing problems of vagrants, wanderers from other parishes and disabled soldiers, and also of affairs relating to apprentices and workmen, street crime and the regulation of all local matters

A brief from a Quarter Sessions court, 1893.
Lincolnshire Archives

pertaining to the social order. The magistrates were first created as a fresh form of the previous 'Keeper of the Peace' and it is no accident that they appeared and were more clearly defined at a time of massive social crisis. The Black Death of 1348 and the horrendous years of famine previous to that, along with other epidemics and social revolt, made the year of 1361 one of the most significant in British legal history. It was followed by an Act which set up Quarter Sessions the next year. The immediate context was one of the widespread threat of violence and roving gangs across the land.

Quarter Sessions dealt with capital offences until the 1660s and from that time there were also an increasing number of petty sessions, hearings often dealing with many of the matters the Quarter Sessions normally handled. The everyday offences before the magistrates were misdemeanours, crimes that could be tried without a jury. Of course, they were the place where the first appearance of a person arrested for a felony would appear too, the cases being handed on to the assize hearing that came up next on the calendar.

The magistrates receive an appeal. Lincolnshire Archives

In the nineteenth century, many local offences were dealt with by police courts, which were yet another form of petty session, but the quarter sessions went on; the centre of the great law machine in the heart of the social upheavals of the Industrial Revolution, when massive threats of riot and disorder were everywhere in the first three decades, in which Luddites, 'Captain Swing' rural crime and the Chartist movement added to the burden of the justices. In an issue of *The Strand* magazine in 1891, a feature article explained the situation then:

In the large cities, such as Newcastle and Liverpool, there are stipendiary magistrates, who are appointed by the Home Secretary at the instance of the local town council, which provides their salaries. The metropolis is divided for the purpose of police administration into various districts, every police court having two magistrates, each of whom sits three days a week, the busiest days being Mondays and Tuesdays. The work of the London police magistrates is of an exceedingly diversified character, consisting principally of charges of drunkenness, petty larceny, assaults on the police or on private individuals . . .

We tend to find out more about a particular magistrate when there are bundles of papers in archives concerning a troublesome or extended case. A typical example is in the wranglings over licensing of inns and beer houses in the last few decades of the nineteenth century. For instance, there was the case of Ann Robinson, who took on the local magistrates and won.

In 1893 Mrs Ann Robinson, a widow, kept a public house in Market Rasen, Lincolnshire. At that time in England, there was no shortage of inns, pubs and beer shops. In fact, the small market town where she ran her business had an excess of them. But she began to have some problems, and the police took action. Her pub, the *White Lion Inn*, had a taproom which attracted the worst sort of men, notably tramps and apprentices out for a good time.

Running a country inn at that time was one of the most demanding occupations for anyone, let alone a widow. A series of drawings published in 1879 depict scenes from the life of a public house: one picture shows a group of around twenty people – men, women and children – waiting for a public house to open; another shows 'men, women and children drinking gin' in a pub and the last shows a drunkard causing havoc. The illustrations in *Punch* for the later Victorian years often show violent drunks and pubs in upheaval as the gin and beer have done their work. Only seven years before Ann had her license withdrawn, a landlady of a pub in Barton upon Humber had to stand by while a brawl broke out in her bar: pots were smashed and when a constable came to sort it out he was beaten up.

In June 1892, Ann was convicted of permitting drunkenness on her premises and fined £3 with costs. Again, she was later convicted of serving liquor to drunks. The law clearly stated that 'The holder of a justice's licence shall not permit drunkenness or any violent, quarrelsome or riotous conduct to take place on his (or her) premises, nor sell intoxicating liquor to a drunken person.' The trade had always been an awkward one for the landlord or landlady: in 1861 a new beer house had opened in the village of Navenby, for instance, and on the first night, the unfortunate landlord had a fight on his premises involving three brothers, and had to call the police. He started with a big black mark in the minds of the local constabulary. The local police took against Ann Robinson and three officers stated at the Great Grimsby Quarter Sessions that there were several reasons why her licence should be removed. They listed these charges:

- There was no stabling at the inn.
- Within ten yards of her premises there were two other fully licensed pubs, and only twelve yards away there was a beer shop.
- There had been the two convictions against her.
- Police officers had stated that the place was 'badly conducted'.

Sergeant John Parker stated that he had noted that the taproom was 'the resort of apprentice boys' and Constable James Cooke said that he had never seen the landlady in the taproom. He complained: 'It has been left to the care of a young servant girl.'

The magistrates wrote to give notice that Ann Robinson's licence was to be withdrawn. That was enough for Ann: she was going to fight the decision. She went to her solicitor and a campaign began to clear her name and have her licence retained. It was a time when the licensing of pubs and beer shops was in the news. Up and down the land, in special quarter sessions called 'brewster sessions', licensing had been in the news. In August that year in Blackburn, the Chief Constable had objected to licence renewal of seventeen out of forty places of refreshment; he won his case, and in addition, another nine businesses, including an off-licence and five more beer houses were refused licences.

The late Victorian years and the Edwardian period saw a rapid increase in beer shops. Workers often had a drink in the early morning on the way to work, and then stopped off again for a beer, or more, on the way home. Ann Robinson was trading at that time, with hot competition down the road, and as a widow, she would have been alone in her fight. But she had very good and talented solicitors. She was sure that the magistrates were being most unfair and took them to court. In the Market Rasen Petty Sessions for October 1893, she appealed, on the basis that insufficient proof was given or tendered before the bench, and that the *White Lion Inn* was not at all badly conducted. Ann was feeling victimised. Amazingly, she was successful, and the justices were ordered to pay £29.14s and 10p 'for the seasonable charges and costs of the said appellant by them sustained and incurred'.

What Ann had done was enlist the help of the brewery in Lincoln with whom she worked. Their man, and the local solicitor, had chased up every charge and reference, even sending a man to check on the stated offences. But there was also an issue on a larger scale. Questions had been asked in Parliament in July that year: the Home Secretary was asked if a Temperance advocate was allowed to sit as a magistrate, and he had answered in the affirmative. Obviously, there were likely to be Temperance men on the benches up and down the land. The Temperance Movement was gaining strength as the beer shops increased, and marches through the towns, in which Temperance banners were held high, were common sights. Taking the pledge was fashionable, although in many cases it was a matter of show rather than resolve.

In 1904, the Licensing Act tackled the question of the proliferation of licensed premises and reduced their number to a considerable extent. There had been statutory licensing of alehouses by justices in England since 1552, and the annual Brewster Sessions had become an institution, dealing with a motley assemblage of licensing cases. The beer shops had arrived after 1830, when the Beer Act was passed; but Ann's place was an inn. What had affected her was the 1872 act which dealt more directly with drunkenness – hence her conviction for selling to a drunkard. We can appreciate the scale of the problem of social drinking when we note that in 1869, according to Paul Jennings, there were 118,500 licences given for premises to sell alcoholic drinks. There was a gradual decline after the 1872 act, and by 1901 there were 'a little under 103,000 licences'.

That national picture places Ann Robinson's fight to remain in business in context: she stood against the tide of repression and reform because she felt that she was the victim of an injustice. The statement resulting from her appeal reads that 'the refusal to renew such licence was contrary to law and inequitable' and so Reverend William Waldo Cooper, Louis Charles Tennyson d'Eyncourt, Cook Holdershaw and Gerard Young esquires would have had to reach into their considerable pockets and pay up. The member of the Tennyson family, Louis Charles, had been a Metropolitan Police magistrate also; he died in 1896. As for Ann, she returned to her work with, undoubtedly, a wonderful feeling of triumph, although we can be sure that she spent some time in the taproom and was more severe with the noisy drunks. But she had been one unusual instance in a national debate. The Bishop of Chester spoke out on the 'drink question' and caused a stir. One correspondent wrote to *The Times* to insist that the much-maligned landlords were actually worthy of a second look, writing that 'The reports presented by the police to the licensing magistrates at the Brewster Sessions now being held furnish pretty conclusive evidence that publicans are by no means what their enemies imagine them to be, but are essentially a law-abiding section of the community.'

This story brings out a great deal about the magistrates involved; they become more visible and more rounded as people because of the furore of course.

The creation of the magistracy

In 1195, the Keepers of the Peace were created. Richard I gave them the task of keeping the peace, applied to everyone over the age of 16. Their powers gradually increased and it became clear to successive authorities that the principle was very useful; so in 1327 there was an Act specifying that 'In every county there shall be assigned good and lawful men to keep the peace.' By 1361 the word 'justice' replaced the word 'keeper'.

The duties of the magistrate, as they were later called, were 'To retrain the offenders, rioters, and all other barators [people who incited public strife], pursue, arrest, take and chastise them according to their trespass or offence, and cause them to be imprisoned and punished according to the law . . . ' As the criminal code was expanded the workload increased, of course; in the first hundred years of the office, as laws proliferated, they even had to preserve young salmon in major rivers; keep a close eye on the powerful trade guilds, and even appoint various persons, including constables, to form the legal functions in a parish or county.

In the Tudor period the magistrates really came into their own, as repressive laws surged from the statutes: there were no less than eleven acts made to try to cope with the problem of vagabonds. Bertram Osborne, author of the standard history of the magistracy, has called the magistrate the 'general factotum of the state'. This began to be utterly accurate as a description, as new offences arrived, and as vogues and trends in crime came along.

Information on magistrates

Finding out about your magistrate ancestor involves a time-consuming task, but it is worth the effort. At the heart of this activity is the *Law List*. This massive annual publication provides lists of magistrates, as does *Whitaker's Almanack*. Both began in the early years of the twentieth century. The latter lists staff at the metropolitan magistrates' courts, together with stipendiary magistrates: in the 1931 edition, for instance, there are sixteen of these. This class of magistrates are full-time, and appointed to act alone. They were formerly barristers or solicitors of at least seven years' standing. They were replaced by the new office of district judge in the 1980s.

Apart from the magistrates who wrote their autobiographies, the people in that office doing the everyday work at the local bench appear in the texts only through quarter sessions records. At archives in County Record Offices and in press reports, their names will appear regularly, but of course, there will only be brief accounts of them.

Exceptions are with reference to earlier times, before the nineteenth century, when a number of these magistrates (many of them being clergymen or local aristocrats) figure in printed versions of quarter sessions as produced by record societies or legal history societies. But there is a resource which is open to all and is accessible online: The Black Sheep Index.com – this provides lists of criminals, police officers and lawyers with dates on which their names appeared in newspapers. When you trace your ancestor in the list, the relevant press cutting may be bought for a small sum. Of course, your local or regional paper may figure in a library index in some areas, and so it will also be possible to trace court reports with accounts of the magistrates and their actions included.

Case studies: Edmund Tew and H Rider Haggard

Tew was rector of Boldon in County Durham between 1735 and his death in 1770. He was born in Northampton and educated in Cambridge, where he began his ministry. His notebook, published by the Surtees Society, is packed with notes on the mundane cases before him. It gives vivid evidence of the kinds of human transgression the local magistrate had to deal with, having a staple diet of assaults, thefts, drunkenness and prostitution.

It was not merely a case of this particular magistrate deciding to log everything: generally, justices were encouraged to keep notebooks, but not many survive. Thanks to the Surtees Society, we have a marvellous edition of this, with notes and index. The social context for this legal work was the area around a number of parishes, and of course coal-mining and shipping were the local industries. There are a few serious offences, meaning that the case was moved on to the assizes, but generally, the matters coming before him were related to violence, damage to property, master and servant arguments and other petty crimes. Very few of the cases that came before Tew actually went to court; there are over a thousand warrants, but the editors of the edition point out that they have traced only twenty-one people from these lists who appeared at assizes and quarter sessions.

The editors also indicate the importance of such notebooks for historians: 'The resulting list provides a picture of the huge number of offended victims who turned to a magistrate for justice, demanding that those who had given offence be forced to answer for their behaviour.'

Typical entries in the notebooks are these:

11th Removed Jane Smith from Monk Wearmouth to the parish of Whickham upon her oath that she was born there and . . . had acquired no other settlement.

24th Granted general warrant against William Bell, brewer of Swalwell for beating Bruising and threatening the life of John Wilson, refiner of iron, at Swalwell.

As JA Sharpe wrote when reviewing this publication: 'Tew's notebook . . . allows us to get into the enforcement of the law on a very local level. It demonstrates how far the process of local administration reached deeply into the lives of the population . . . .' Normally access to the records of daily work undertaken by magistrates is rare indeed, and some of the best insights into the work come from obscure edited texts such as this, but fortunately there are famous people who have also been magistrates and one of these was the novelist, Henry Rider Haggard.

In his book, *A Farmer's Year* (1899), we have accounts of events at the bench in Norfolk and he reflects, for instance, on some petty crimes from June 1898: after hearing a case of egg-stealing, in which a man described as a marine dealer was accused of sending a box of 251 partridge eggs to another dealer. The man was fined a shilling an egg or two months in gaol. Haggard's thoughts on poaching give us an insight into some of the main issues magistrates dealt with. He notes:

'. . . I have on several occasions seen poaching cases dismissed when the evidence would have been thought sufficient to ensure conviction . . . it is extraordinary what an amount of false sentiment is wasted in certain quarters upon poachers, who, for the most part, are very cowardly villains . . .'

On the other hand, in his note for 20 April in the same year, there is a case of lunacy. He writes, in his capacity as the magistrate appointed to be in action in cases under the Lunacy Acts, 'About breakfast time on Sunday morning I was requested by an overseer to attend in a neighbouring village to satisfy myself by personal examination as to the madness of a certain pauper lunatic . . .' He did indeed, and then he signed the orders needed for her removal to an asylum. It was a sad occasion and a huge responsibility for him. He adds, 'It seems that it was not considered advisable that the patient should remain longer out of proper control, so, as she could not be removed without a magistrate's order, I was followed to the church.'

Magistrates therefore have always had to be capable of sorting out all kinds of matters, and your ancestor doing this valuable work will have had to do many things comparable to Rider Haggard, but the search for details may be harder of course.

Chapter Five
A SURVEY OF SOURCES I

The Surtees Society and the Selden Society

The Surtees Society was created in 1834, in honour of Robert Surtees, who died that year. He was the author of *The History and Antiquities of the County Palatine of Durham* (1816–1840). It represents the scholarly society which takes an interest in provincial records across the centuries and reprints important texts, edited and indexed. In the society's lists there are several volumes relating to legal history. The original purpose was 'To have for its object the publication of edited manuscripts illustrative of the intellectual, the moral, the religious, and the social condition of those parts of England and Scotland, included on the East between the Humber and the Firth of Forth, and on the West between the Mersey and the Clyde, a region which constituted the Ancient Kingdom of Northumberland.'

The Society, already mentioned as the publishers of the Tew justicing book, have also produced such items as the *Northumberland Eyre Roll for 1293, Durham Quarter Sessions Rolls 1471–1625*, wills and inventories, and substantial biographical volumes. These provide all kinds of contextual information for the understanding of the workings of law in those years and the biographical texts add significantly to our knowledge of administrators and functionaries through the centuries.

The Selden Society takes its name from John Selden (1584–1654) who entered Clifford's Inn in 1602 and then the Inner Temple two years later. He was called to the Bar, but also wrote some significant works on the law, notably *History of Tythes* (1617), a work which was suppressed as it offended the churchmen of the time. Selden entered political history when he took the role of counsel to John Hampden, the

MP who was openly in opposition to the King in his demand for ship money. Selden was on the committee which studied the offence on the part of King Charles II in impinging on parliamentary privileges.

More directly relevant to family historians is the publication programme of the Selden Society. This was established in 1887 by the great legal historian, FW Maitland. The Society specialises in printed editions of all kinds of texts from legal history, and from the beginning it has had the support of the Law Society and the Inns of Court; 150 volumes of material have been published, covering law reports, judges' notebooks and all kinds of primary sources in law.

Selden publications include lists of several categories of legal professionals, including the order of serjeants-at-law, King's Counsel members and judges. Some examples will show how useful these resources are to the family historian. First, serjeants-at-law, this is the kind of information there:

Nov. 1495:   John Mordaunt
Thomas Oxenbrigge
Richard Higham
Thomas Frowyk
Robert Constable
John Yaxley

The supporting material and notes, by JH Baker, provide more details.

There is also a volume on the admissions to Barnard's Inn, covering the years 1620–1869, with this kind of entry:

5 May 1858 GEORGE LEWIS PARKIN
Nominated and then asked if he wanted to become a member in April, 1858 before being admitted without probation. Lends the Society £1,000 in Mar. 1869 to pay debt owed to Pughs. Moves in May 1871 that the arms of the antients not already in the Hall should be placed there. Moves that the Hall should be repaired. Feb. 1872, in charge of wine supply . . . Principal 1880–3. Reported dead May 1885.

The volumes of professional listings also have explanatory notes, and these are needed for much of the rather arcane information. For instance, the volume on the King's Counsel explains that the office originated in 1604, and that these men were appointed by Letters Patent under the Great Seal. These documents have been in English since 1733. The Great Seal is under the supervision of the Lord Chancellor and is used to sign treaties with foreign states, and for elections.

The lists are bare but with the essential information, such as:

Price, Gruffyd
App. 28 Jan. 1771
D. 27 July 1787

Coroners

It is not hard to find records of what coroners did, even as far back as 1349, when we know from coroners' rolls that 'Inquest was taken before the coroners of the city of York concerning the death of William Yonge, slain at York at twilight . . . ' Then, at the end of the brief report, we have the name of the coroner: 'Robert fled forthwith, and had no chattels . . . William was viewed and buried by Thomas of Lincoln, the coroner.'

This type of information may be found in the coroners' rolls, some published by the Selden Society, and some by the Sussex Archaeological Collections (Vol. XCV, 1957).

From 1752 to 1860 coroners had to file their inquests at the Quarter Sessions, so these will be in the Quarter Sessions records at record offices. The quickest way to locate these is through Access to Archives (A2A) as an internet search. A standard volume which has listings of holdings is *Coroners' Records in England and Wales* by J Gibson and C Rogers, and this has details of coroners' districts. Coroners' records more than seventy-five years old are usually open; and in cases from earlier times, the inquests would have been given to the judge at the assizes.

There have also been coroners' records from other jurisdictions, and these are listed in the research guide at TNA website. These have, for example, lists of records left at the King's Bench prison between 1746

Sheriffs, &c., of Counties in Scotland. 253

LIST OF SHERIFFS, SHERIFFS-SUBSTITUTE, SHERIFF-CLERKS, AND FISCALS OF COUNTIES IN SCOTLAND.

Counties.	Sheriffs.	Sheriffs-Substitute.	Sheriff-Clerks.	Procurators-Fiscal.
ABERDEEN	A. L. M'Clure, K.C... 1,050	A. J. Louttit Laing. 1,100 / J. Dewar Dallas 1,100	James Hunter.....	Thos. Maclennan.
ARGYLL—	John L. Wark, K.C... 700			
Dunoon		James B. Ballingall. 900	D. A. Allan........	A. R. Nimmo.
Campbeltown	....	John M. Campbell .. 700		J. M. Mactaggart.
Oban		T. A. Menzies 700	....	D. M. MacKinnon.
AYR—	W. L. Mackenzie, K.C. 700			
Ayr		J. R Haldane 600	J. Hamilton	R. D. Macmillan.
Kilmarnock	....	A. M. Laing 900		W. J. Robertson.
BANFF	See Aberdeen	John W. More 900	R. G. Shirreffs	James Kissock.
BERWICK	See Roxburgh	H. Burn-Murdoch.... 700	Jas. Somerville	R. G. Johnson.
BUTE	See Renfrew	J. B. Ballingall...... 700	T. W. Alexander ..	W. Grant.
CAITHNESS	Alex. Maitland, K.C. 775	Thomas Trotter ... 700	Robert Bruce	Peter Sinclair.
CLACKMANNAN	See Stirling	J Dean Leslie...... 950	Douglas McGregor.	J. B. Haig.
DUMBARTON	See Stirling	A. J. P. Menzies ... 900	Daniel M'Bride....	H. L. Yeudall.
DUMFRIES........	Rt. Hon. Baron Kinross, K.C......700	J. G. Brand 900	John McBurnie ...	R. Y. Mackay.
EDINBURGH	Chas. H. Brown, K.C. 1,500	R. L. Orr, K.C. ......1,400 / E. W. Neish ....1,200 / J. G. Jameson 1,000	And. Harrison ...	W. Horne.
ELGIN OT MORAY	See Inverness	C. R. A. Howden.... 800	John Foster.	D. A. Shinch.
FIFE—	J. C. Fenton, K.C. ...800			
Cupar..............		Dudley Stuart 1,000	Robt. J. Davidson	Geo. Brander.
Dunfermline	....	F. A. Umpherston. 1,000	....	R. J. Waugh.
FORFAR—	George Morton, K.C. 800			
Forfar		S. McDonald, C.M.G., D.S.O. 800	C. J. Bisset	Thos. Hart.
Dundee.............	....	R. C. Malcolm 1,000	C. J. Bisset	J. R. Archibald.
HADDINGTON	See Edinburgh	J. G. Jameson	Andrew Hamilton	Thos. W. Todrick.
INVERNESS	George Watt, K.C. ... 800			
Inverness.........		John P. Grant, M.C.. 800	Arch. A. Chisholm	Wm. Anderson.
Fort William	....	Alexander Steedman 700	....	Dun. Macniven.
Portree	....	W. R Garson 750	....	W. R. D. Macmillan.
Lochmaddy......	....	W. R. Garson..........	....	A. C. F. Davidson.
KINCARDINE	See Aberdeen	A. J. Louttit Laing.......... / J. Dewar Dallas..........	James B. Cunning- ham.	M. A. Hamilton.
KINROSS	See Fife	F. A. Umpherston	D. A. R. Cuthbert	John S. Soutar.
KIRKCUDBRIGHT	See Dumfries	W. G. Skinner 900	James Warnock ...	Jas. Williamson.
LANARK—	A. O. M. Mackenzie, K.C.			
Glasgow	.... [2,000	J. A. Welsh ....1,200 / D. S. Macdiarmid ..1,200 / John Swan Mercer. 1,200 / W. J. Robertson ...1,200 / John Bartholomew..1,200 / Marcus Dods.......1,200 / W. Boyd Berry....1,200	Robert George Slorach.	J. D. Strathearn.
Lanark	....	G. W. Wilton, K.C...1,200	....	Wm. Tennant.
Hamilton..........	....	A. R. Brown, K.C. ...1,200 / Jas. Macdonald, K.C. 1,200	....	J. Adair.
Airdrie	....	T. D. King Murray..1,200		D. J. Henry.
LINLITHGOW	See Edinburgh	J. A. T. Robertson 1,200	A. P. Simpson, W.S.	Geo. S. Macnight.
NAIRN	See Inverness	C. R. A. Howden	A. Robertson, S.S.C.	James Lamb.
ORKNEY	See Caithness	George Brown......	Jn. White........	James Begg.
PEEBLES	See Edinburgh	(vacant)	Ro. Lendrem Ainslie	J. W. Buchan.
PERTH	J.O.S. Sandeman,K.C. 750	G. D. Valentine 1,000	John Dickson......	Martin L. Howman.
RENFREW—	J. M. Irvine, K.C. ... 800			
Paisley		A. M. Hamilton, K.C. 800	A. F. Lochhead	E. W. Paterson.
Greenock		Robert Hendry 900		W. Guthrie Young.
ROSS AND CROMARTY—	Jas. Mackintosh, K.C. 700			
Dingwall		Hon. H. D. Gordon.. 800	Alex. Ross	W. R. T. Middleton.
Stornoway	....	J. G. Burns......... 700		C. G. Mackenzie.
ROXBURGH	J. M. Hunter, K.C. .. 750	Ronald H. Baillie .. 750	A. P. Oliver	Sydney Hilson.
SELKIRK	See Roxburgh	(vacant)	T. M. Kinnaird ...	John Pollok.
STIRLING—	J.R. N. Macphail, K.C. 800			
Stirling............		J. Dean Leslie...........	J. A. Proctor......	Charles C. Cheyne.
Falkirk		A. T. Robertson ..1,100		J. G. Morrison.
SUTHERLAND	See Ross and Cromarty ..	J. W. Forbes 700	John McCrone	R. S. Henderson.
WIGTOWN	See Dumfries...........	W. G. Skinner;......	James Warnock ...	H. C. Todd.
Stranraer	....			Alex. Aitken.
ZETLAND	See Caithness	J. R. Gibb 700	A. Sutherland	L. H. Mathewson.

In Scotland the principal local court is the Sheriff Court. The Judge Ordinary is the Sheriff-Substitute, and the Sheriff is an Appeal Judge. The jurisdiction of the Sheriff Court is both civil and criminal. In civil questions the jurisdiction is unlimited in regard to the money value of the cause. On the criminal side the Court has cognizance of all serious crime with the exception of murder and three other charges, but the power of punishment is limited to fine and imprisonment; it does not extend to penal servitude.

The Sheriff Clerk is the Clerk of the Sheriff Court, and his duties correspond nearly to those of a Registrar in the English Courts. Prosecutions are conducted by Crown officials at the public expense; the Lord Advocate and his deputes prosecute in the High Court; the Procurators-Fiscal in the Sheriff Court. The Convener of the sheriffs is Sheriff Alexander L. M'Clure, Aberdeen. The Address of the *Secretary of the Sheriff's-Substitute Assoc.* is County Buildings, Ayr.

List of sheriffs published in Whitaker's Almanack, 1931. *Author's collection* and 1839, and records from the palatinate courts. The latter were Chester, Lancaster and Durham. The Chester palatinate court was abolished in 1830, Durham in 1876, and the court of Lancaster the same year.

In the twentieth century, coroners were listed in *Whitaker's Almanack*, with this kind of information:

COUNTY OF LONDON CORONERS
Western District: Edwin Smith
Coroner's office, Battersea Coroner's Court, Sheepcote Lane, Battersea, S. W.

Almanacs and biographical reference works

The starting point for so much research into legal ancestors is in bio-graphical works. The *Law Lists* have been produced since 1775 and they provide a very useful first step. The National Archives has a set covering 1799–1976, and the Guildhall Library also has some early volumes. It has to be said that there are some reservations: sometimes there are men listed who never went to a court, and from 1790 the only people listed are those who had a certificate to practise merely for that year. The volumes up to 1861 do not have the dates of ad-mission to the law, either, so there are limitations. However, the listings are useful, as in this example:

ABERDEEN
Adam, Thomson and Ross, advocates, solicitors, notaries. 6, Bon Accord Square. Solicitors to Northern Assurance Co . . . Telegraphic address, "Terrace, Aberdeen."

In contrast, almanacs provide simply names and locations, as in the residents of the Inns of Court with all their roles, and there the reader may be informed that, for instance in 1836, the registrar of the Court of Admiralty was Daniel Pineau and the Lord Chief Justice at Common Pleas was the Rt Hon John Doherty. However, they are the best place to look as a first step in research, as addresses are given in some cases, as well as names and qualifications.

1931.

THE LAW LIST:

COMPRISING THE

JUDGES AND OFFICERS

OF THE

Courts of Justice;

COUNSEL, SPECIAL PLEADERS, CONVEYANCERS, SOLICITORS,

PROCTORS, NOTARIES, &c.,

IN ENGLAND AND WALES,

THE CIRCUITS, JUDGES, AND REGISTRARS

OF THE

COUNTY COURTS;

METROPOLITAN AND STIPENDIARY MAGISTRATES

OFFICIAL RECEIVERS UNDER THE BANKRUPTCY & COMPANIES ACTS.

COLONIAL AND FOREIGN JUDGES AND LAWYERS,

&c., &c.

Published, so far as relates to Certificated Solicitors practising in England and Wales, by the Authority of The Law Society.

COMPILED SO FAR AS RELATES TO

Special Pleaders, Conveyancers, Solicitors, Proctors,

and Notaries,

BY

CHARLES CONNOLLY GALLAGHER,

CONTROLLER OF STAMPS AND REGISTRAR OF COMPANIES

And Published by the Authority of the Commissioners of Inland Revenue

LONDON:

STEVENS AND SONS, LIMITED,

119 & 120, CHANCERY LANE.

Law Publishers.

Title page of The Law List, *1931. Author's collection*

THE LAW LIST.]   [xi] [*Judges of County Courts.*

JUDGES OF COUNTY COURTS.

Name. His Honour Judge	Date of Appointment.	Circuit No.	Address
A. Gwynne-James.	Jan., 1900	52	7, cavendish-cres., Bath.
Hon. W. B. Lindley	Sept.,1902	57	corfe-house, Taunton.
E. Harington .	Nov.,1905	45	66, onslow - gardens, s.w.7.
A. H. Ruegg, K.C..	Sept.,1907	21 & 26	highfields, Uttoxeter.
S. A. Hill Kelly .	Jan., 1910	42	Bloomsbury county court, 209, gt. portland-st. w. 1.
A. R. Cluer . .	July, 1911	39	county court, great-prescot-st., whitechapel E. 1.
A. Spencer Hogg .	Apr., 1913	48	Lambeth county court, cleaver-st. S.E. 11.
Sir Wm. Moore Cann.	Mar., 1914	50	the governor's-ho., Lewes.
Sir A. A. Tobin, K.C.	May, 1915	44	82, st. martin's-la., w.c.2.
Barnard Lailey,K.C.	Oct., 1916	51	county court,Portsmouth.
A. Parsons, K.C. .	May, 1917	54	county court, Bristol.
Ivor Bowen, K.C. .	Feb., 1918	28	county court, Shrewsbury.
J. D. Crawford .	Mar., 1918	38	the orchard, wellesleyrd., Gunnersbury w. 4.
Rowland Rowlands, LL.B.	May, 1918	30	clevis cottage, Newton, Porthcawl.
H. G. Farrant .	Oct., 1918	35	3, newnham-walk, Cambridge.
R. E. Moore . .	May, 1919	47	eliot vale-house, Blackheath, S.E. 3.
H. L. Tebbs . .	Aug.,1919	25	county court, Wolverhampton.
R. W. Turner .	Oct., 1919	34 &c.	82, st. martin's-la., w.c.2.
T. M. Snagge .	Oct., 1919	43	Marylebone county court, marylebone-rd. N.W. 1.
A. Hyslop Maxwell.	Feb., 1920	55	cumloden, wimborne-rd. Bournemouth.
J. R. Randolph,K.C.	Mar., 1921	36	1, church-walk, Oxford.
Harold Chaloner Dowdall, K.C.	May, 1921	6	40,stanley-road,Hoylake, Cheshire.
C. Herbert-Smith .	Aug.,1921	32	cedar - grange, Hethersett, Norwich.
F. E. Bradley, M.A.	Oct., 1921	4	8, balmoral - road, St. Annes-on-Sea.
Gerald de la Pryme Hargreaves.	Mar., 1922	37	West London county court, 43, north-endroad w. 14.
W. L. Richards .	July, 1922	7	woodfield, Hoole, Chester.
W. J. Lias . .	Oct., 1922	59	county court, Plymouth.
G. H. Higgins .	Jan., 1923	46	county court, Brentford.

Judges of the County Courts published in The Law List. *Author's collection*

Whitaker's Almanack, in contrast, for twentieth-century research, has a long section on 'Law and Justice' which lists the judiciary, judges of circuits, composition of industrial and ecclesiastical courts, county court judges, recorders, metropolitan and stipendiary magistrates, and all the principal posts held in Scotland. This is very detailed, as in this entry from the 1931 edition on the King's Bench Division:

Justices	Apptd.	Age Jan. 1	
Hon. Sir Horace F Avory	1910	79	
Hon. Sir Thomas G Horridge		1912	73
Hon. Sir Sidney A T Rowlatt		1912	68

The principal survey of all main biographical sources is Guy Holborn's *Sources of Biographical Information on Past Lawyers*. The writer is a librarian at Lincoln's Inn Library, and the material covers over 500 sources, in England and in Wales. The book covers sources relating to barristers, inns of court, serjeants, attorneys and solicitors, but firms and individuals are left out. To complement this, there is AWB Simpson's *Biographical Dictionary of the Common Law* (1984). This includes all kinds of people, and the entries are quite substantial, as in this for Henry Challis:

Challis, Henry William, Conveyancer and author (4.1.1841–1.4.1898) B. Brixton; ed. Merton Coll. Oxford; BA 1864, MA 1871 bar. IT 1876

Challis was one of the last outstanding nineteenth-century conveyancers. A Catholic convert inspired by J M Newman, he worked for some years as a teacher of moral philosophy at Edgbaston, and was 35 when he began at the Bar. His *Law of Real Property, chiefly in relation to conveyancing* (1885), which remains a classic of its kind, gave the law student a much needed standard textbook . . .

There are also other possibilities, shown most clearly perhaps in the publications of Judy Slinn. She has written several books tracing the history of firms, such as *Linklaters and Paines: the First One Hundred*

ENGLAND AND WALES—*continued*

STRATFORD-UPON-AVON, WARWICK.

PARKER (GEOFFREY) & PEACOCK (V. Geoffrey Parker, LL.B., 1933, *C.O.* ; J. Nevil Peacock, 1948, *C.O.*).

Solicitors and Commissioners for Oaths

ADDRESS : Scholars Lane, Stratford-upon-Avon. Branch Offices : Southam Street, Kineton (Wednesdays only) and 30, Church Street, Shipston-on-Stour.

TELEPHONE : Stratford-upon-Avon 2051 ; Kineton 373 ; Shipston 304.

SUNDERLAND, CO. DURHAM

HUTTON, QUENET & FUNNELL (William McDonald Quenet, 1920, *C.O.*, Not. Pub. ; Harold Vernon Cecil Funnell, 1940, *C.O.*, Not. Pub.).

Solicitors, Commissioners for Oaths and Notaries Public

ADDRESS : Sunniside Chambers, 40, West Sunniside, Sunderland.

TELEPHONE : Sunderland 4378.

TELEGRAPHIC ADDRESS : " Sunderland 4378."

LONDON AGENTS : Taylor, Jelf & Co., Amberley House, Norfolk Street, Strand, W.C.2.

SURBITON, SURREY

MADDIN (C. A.) & CO. (W. E. Farquharson, Clerk to the Commissioners of Taxes (Division of Kingston and Elmbridge), 1943 ; Eric Dodds, Clerk to the Justices (Borough of Richmond), 1930 ; John A. Whittaker, 1931).

Solicitors and Commissioners for Oaths

ADDRESS : Lloyds Bank Chambers, Surbiton ; Midland Bank Chambers, Surbiton ; and 1, Southampton Place, Bloomsbury Square, London, W.C. 1.

TELEPHONE : Elmbridge 2741, 2742 and 4001.

SWANAGE, DORSET

HUMPHRIES, KIRK & MILLER (Christopher Munro Humphries, M.A. (Oxon.), 1923, *C.O.*, Clerk to Commissioners of Taxes ; Harry Kirk, M.A. (Oxon.), LL.B. (Lond.), 1936, *C.O.*, Town Clerk, Wareham ; John Penn Sherbrooke, 1944, *C.O.*).

Solicitors and Commissioners for Oaths
Members of Law Society

ADDRESS : 12a, Institute Road, Swanage ; and at Wareham

TELEPHONE : Swanage 2385 ; Wareham 214.

LONDON AGENTS : Barnes & Butler.

SLADE & WEST (Christopher Munro Humphries, M.A. (Oxon.), 1923, *C.O.*, Clerk to Commissioners of Taxes ; Harry Kirk, M.A. (Oxon.), LL.B. (Lond.), 1936, *C.O.*, Town Clerk, Wareham ; John Penn Sherbrooke, 1944, *C.O.*).

Solicitors and Commissioners for Oaths
Members of Law Society

ADDRESS : 15, Institute Road, Swanage.

TELEPHONE : Swanage 2390.

LONDON AGENTS : Kimbers & Co.

SWANSEA, GLAM.

JAMES (T. W.) & CO. (Mrs. A. Menna Morris, LL.B., 1935, *C.O.* ; Philip M. Cowling, 1945, *C.O.* ; James W. Mallows, 1949).

Solicitors and Commissioners for Oaths

ADDRESS : 95, Walter Road, Swansea ; and at Tenby, Pembrokeshire.

TELEPHONE : Swansea 57831/2 ; Tenby 57.

TELEGRAPHIC ADDRESS : " James, Solicitors, Swansea."

LONDON AGENTS : Waterhouse & Co.

STRICK & BELLINGHAM (Roger Kirril Bellingham, 1921, Not. Pub. ; James William Charles Knoyle, M.A. (Oxon.), 1949).

Solicitors and Notaries Public

ADDRESS : 29, Fisher Street, Swansea.

TELEPHONE : Swansea 3539.

TELEGRAPHIC ADDRESS : " Strick Bellingham, Swansea."

LONDON AGENTS : Tamplin, Joseph & Flux.

The Empire Law List, *from* The Law List, *a typical entry. Author's collection*

THE
EMPIRE LAW LIST
1952/53

CIRCULATED TO MEMBERS OF THE LEGAL PROFESSION
THROUGHOUT THE WORLD

BUTTERWORTH & CO. (Publishers) Ltd., Bell Yard, Temple Bar,
London, W.C. 2

AFRICA:
BUTTERWORTH & CO. (AFRICA) Ltd., 1, Lincoln's Court (P.O. Box 792), Masonic Grove,
DURBAN, NATAL.
AUSTRALIA:
BUTTERWORTH & CO. (AUSTRALIA) Ltd., 8, O'Connell St., Sydney, N.S.W.
240, Queen St., BRISBANE, QLD. 430, Bourke St., MELBOURNE, VIC.
CANADA:
BUTTERWORTH & CO. (CANADA) Ltd., 1367, Danforth Avenue, TORONTO, 6, ONT.
NEW ZEALAND:
BUTTERWORTH & CO. (AUSTRALIA) Ltd., 49/51, Ballance Street, WELLINGTON.
35, High Street, AUCKLAND.

Frontispiece for The Empire Law List, *1952/53. Author's collection and Fifty Years.* As is illustrated by my case study in chapter 6 in which a Lincoln firm is profiled, this is one of the least appreciated sources for lawyer ancestors, and the packages of materials at County Record Offices offer immense potential for family history researchers. This element of family research reveals the everyday chores of solicitors and barristers, through all kinds of records, including diaries, year books and letters. There is no better way to shed light on the lives of legal professionals in their encounters with people, issues, court process and indeed all the more interesting sometimes are the simply human details, as in one diary which has on one page a list of appointments and on the next page the note 'the ale barrel opened today'.

Scotland.]   [1590]   [THE LAW LIST.

THE LAW LIST.]   [1591]   [*Scotland.*

SCOTLAND.

*Advocates, Solicitors, Commissioners, &c.**

** The names in *Italics* are those of the Agents or Correspondents, whose address may be found by referring to the list of London Solicitors.

Scottish Solicitors Practising in London.

Findlay, McClure & Co., Privy Council agents, and Scottish solicitors and notaries, commissioners for affidavits for Scotland and for the Union of South Africa; secretaries, Surgical and Medical Protection Union of London, Limited, Law and General Assets Co., Limited, *atlantic-house,* 45, *holborn-viaduct,* London, E.C. 1, and at 86, *st. vincent-street,* Glasgow. Telephone, 7430 Holborn.

ABERDEEN.

Adam, Thomson & Ross, advocates, solicitors, notaries, commissioners for oaths, 6, *bon accord-square,* solicitors to Northern Assurance Co., Ltd., Aberdeen Market Co., Ltd., Incorporated Trades of Aberdeen, Engineering Employers' Federation, Aberdeen Shipbuilders' Association, &c. Telegraphic address, "Terrace, Aberdeen."

Bain, Richard W. K., M.A., F.R.S.G.S. (firm Youngson & Bain), advocate, solicitor and conveyancer, notary public and probate agent, and commissioner for oaths for New Zealand, &c., 8, *union-terrace.*   *Ashurst, Morris, Crisp & Co.*

Cooper (Patrick) & Son, advocates, conveyancers, solicitors, notaries, commissioners for oaths (Patrick Cooper, M.A., member of the Law Society of England, John Russell Cooper, B.A. cantab.), 12, *bon accord-square.* Telegrams, "Security, Aberdeen"; telephone, 149.

Davidson & Garden, advocates, solicitors and notaries, 12, *dee-street.* Telephone, 3176; telegrams, "Davgar, Aberdeen."   *Torr & Co.*

Duncan, M. M., C.M.G. (advocate 1891), local agent for the Board of Trade (firm Peterkin & Duncans), 21, *golden-sq.* Telegrams, "Peterkin."   *Stibbard, Gibson & Co.*

Duncan, W. O., N.P. (advocate 1890) (firm Peterkin & Duncans), 21, *golden-sq.* Telegrams, "Peterkin."   *Stibbard, Gibson & Co.*

* The fee for insertion must be paid not later than December 31st.

ABERDEEN—*continued.*

Edmonds & Ledingham, advocates, solicitors, notaries and commissioners for oaths, 1, *golden-sq.,* solicitors to City of Aberdeen Land Association, City of Aberdeen Property and General Investment Trust, Ltd., Incorporated Trades of Aberdeen, &c. (A. Martineau, B.A. cantab., J. H. Edwards, LL.B. (Lecturer on Procedure and Evidence in the University of Aberdeen), G. Robb and R. M. Ledingham, LL.B.). Telegraphic address, "Edmonds, Aberdeen."

Hunter & Gordon, advocates, solicitors, notaries, and commissioners for oaths and affidavits, agents Aberdeen Property Investment Building Society, etc., etc., 222, *union-st.*

Paull & Williamsons, advocates, solicitors, members of the Law Society of England, and commissioners for oaths and affidavits, investment-house, 6, *union-row.* Telegrams, "Investment, Aberdeen"; telephones, 17 and 18.

Peterkin, C. D., C.B.E., Glasgow Guardian Society (firm Peterkin & Duncans), 21, *golden-sq.* Telegrams, "Peterkin."   *Stibbard, Gibson & Co.*

AYR.

Lockhart, John, W. & G., solicitors and notaries, *bank-chambs.,* 211, *high-st.*

DUNDEE.

Morrison, Frank Halley (Sturrock & Morrison), town clerk of Newport, secretary for the Sir John Leng Educational Trust, secretary Dundee branch of National Federation of Master Painters in Scotland, 10, *whitehall-st.,* and at Newport, Fife.

Pattullo & Donald, J. & H., solicitors and notaries public, 1, *bank-st.* Telegraphic address, "Semper—Dundee," telephone 5085.

EDINBURGH.

Aitken, Alfred Niven Gillies, s.s.c., member of the Law Society U.K., commissioner for oaths for Natal, the Provinces of Nova Scotia, Alberta and New Brunswick (firm Aitken, Methuen & Aikman), 37, *queen-st.*

The Law List: *entries for solicitors, Scotland. Author's collection*

There is also another law list, and this is an extremely valuable resource if your ancestor served abroad in the British Empire. This is *The Empire Law List*, and it does include law firms in Great Britain as well as abroad. A typical example is this from the 1950 edition:

Swanage, Dorset
Humphries, Kirk and Miller (Christopher Munro Humphries M.A. (Oxon.) C.O. Clerk to the Commissioners of Taxes; Harry Kirk M.A. (Oxon.) LL.B (London) 1936, Town Clerk, Wareham; John Penn Sherbrooke, 1944 C.O. [C.O. is Commissioner for Oaths.])

Case Study: A Leeds coroner, John Cooper Malcolm

Thanks to local historians and obscure monographs, there is a vast literature on legal ancestors across Britain, and these publications give us an insight into the lives of ancestors in various public professions. Such an example is the research by Sylvia Barnard into the Leeds coroner, John Cooper Malcolm, who served in that post for almost forty-five years. He was born in Leeds, dying at the age of 91 on 24 August 1923. He was elected coroner in September 1876. He had indeed had a busy life: the estimate is that he had conducted at least 25,000 inquests in his career, and on one occasion he sat twenty-two times in the day.

It is possible to learn a great deal about coroners and their lives and duties from this example; Malcolm was qualified for the post as he was a solicitor and had been practising in Leeds for many years at the time he applied for the coroner post. At his retirement he was interviewed by the *Leeds Mercury* and there he referred to the traditional venue of the inn as the scene of an inquest: 'Publicans were usually at great pains to make the coroner's jury comfortable, and the most that the innkeepers in Leeds got was a fee of five shillings for their trouble. Certain it is that in the old-fashioned inns, juries were made more comfortable than they sometimes are in the vestries and school rooms where the inquests have been held since.'

The foundation handbook for coroners is a book written by a

lawyer called Jervis, and this is known as 'Jervis on Coroners'. In that book, the explanation of the election of a coroner, as at 1854, is that an affidavit of death and a petition for a writ called *de coronatore eligendo* [choosing a coroner] had to be signed. Of course, this was normally after the death of the previous coroner, but coroners were sacked. As Jervis jokes: 'Lying in prison for twelve months has also been adjudged good grounds for removing a coroner.'

The men who applied for the post back in 1876 had to be financially secure, and they could be town councillors, but the important point was that they had to live no more than 2 miles beyond the town or city boundaries. Since the 1835 Municipal Corporations Act, the situation had been that the town councillors elected the coroner. There were three coroners for Leeds in the Victorian period, and the first was George Emsley who also was a qualified solicitor; he had succeeded John Blackburn.

Malcolm, in his long career, had to deal with these main categories of deaths: discoveries of corpses (many would be from a long time ago); suicides; street, domestic and industrial accidents; deaths from natural causes; murder and manslaughter. Before Malcolm's time, an inquest held in an inn was certainly well publicised, as in this report form 1866:

The deceased body was exhibited at a public house, where her husband happened to be among the throng going to gawp at it. This public display could certainly prove to be an effective means of identification. Notice the dull, drab clothing described, despite the beads and flounces . . . . Elizabeth, who according to the burial register was 45, must have looked like a frumpish old woman. (*Leeds Mercury* 23 May 1866)

Chapter Six
A SURVEY OF SOURCES II

The National Archives (TNA)

For tracing attorneys and solicitors, the first location of interest is at the material relating to the admission roll books, referenced at TNA at series numbers KB172, CP11, E4, CP70 and CP72, created after the 1728 Attorneys and Solicitors Act, which stated that these professions should have a five-year period of service as clerks under articles. KB172 is for the King's Bench (1729–1875) and E4 is for the Court of Common Pleas. The men involved took an oath and their names were placed on a roll. In addition, there are affidavits of execution of articles of clerkship, after another Act in 1749; these details are on registers, listing the articles and the firms to which they relate. The additional interest here is that the names of parents and guardians are also listed. After 1785 there had to be an annual certificate of admission completed to allow an attorney or solicitor to become established by law. Law lists were then the results of the lists in certificate books.

There are also oath rolls, and these need a little explanation. From the Tudor years to the Victorian period, various social groups were required to take an oath of loyalty to the Crown and to the Church of England. The central oath is the 'Solemn Association' which was established after the accession of William III and all office holders had to take this. There were also oath rolls which were taken abroad in plantations, primarily in several colonies, including Virginia and New York.

With regard to provincial attorneys, after 1830 attorneys at the court of sessions could enrol in the Westminster rolls, and then later in 1843 the Solicitors Act included the palatinate courts and their attorneys (Chester and Durham) were included in the rolls. To complement this, the Law Society has lists from 1843 and some from 1790, of registers of articles.

As stated earlier, although the law lists are the best place to start, the names therein are not always of men who actually practised; for this reason, the court in which the person practised is a more fruitful line of enquiry. The largest number of admissions would have been at the **Court of Common Pleas**, so that should be consulted, and then after 1750, the **King's Bench** becomes the most generally used for admissions. At the Common Pleas, there were registers of articles of clerkship; these are in chronological order, and provide the names of the masters as well of the clerks. In this court, the index volumes are at CP71/1 for 1758–1784 and at CP71/2 for 1785–1867. Articles from the Common Pleas are in the CP5 series.

For the years 1729–1838 the admission papers include details of articles, payment of stamp duties and fiats for admission. A fiat was an order of consent (a warrant) from a judge or other public officer. Of particular interest is the availability of papers relating to some men who did not finish the period of their articles agreement. The admission books, covering the years 1724–1853 are alphabetical; the first series gives addresses and the second series gives the county and the year. Series 1 is in CP70/1 to CP70/4 and series 2 is in CP72/1 to CP72/6. There are also some incomplete materials for registers in the years 1656–1761 and of Welsh attorneys for 1830–1844. These are at CP69/1 and CP72/3 respectively.

For those attorneys at the court of the **King's Bench,** affidavits of execution of articles are at KB105–107. After this process, the affidavit was signed and filed in the Court, dating from 1749, and other series followed. Indexes and registers cover these years and series, arranged alphabetically. But it should be noted that between 1840 and 1849 these are filed according to date of admission, not execution. It may be necessary to relate the information to Law Society lists of admissions.

The registers are at KB170/14 to KB170/22, covering the years from 1749 to 1876, but there are gaps for 1845–1860 where material is missing. Registers of affidavits of execution are at KB170/1 to KB170/13 covering the years 1749 to 1877. There are then three series of Due Execution Articles at KB105/107. Indexes of articles are at KB171/73. There were also rolls of attorneys and these were termed in three categories:

Private rolls: names of admitted attorneys in date order of admission (KB172/1 to 9).

Public or abstract: these do not have full addresses, KB172/10–15, for 'public'; KB172/16 for 'abstract' and KB172/18 for 'Wales rolls' which covered Wales and Chester, listing the men who were admitted to Westminster.

For attorneys admitted to the **Court of Exchequer** and as entry was limited to people selected from limited applications before 1832, the records begin at that date for admission records. These are in series E4/3 which has the years 1833–1855 and then there are rolls of attorneys covering 1830–1875 in the series E4/1 to E4/6. This court also covered Equity and there are books of licences from 1785–1843 listing clerks of the court and solicitors:

Oath rolls: E200/1–2. The second group includes Roman Catholic solicitors, and these cover 1730–1841, the material for 1772–1841 relating to solicitors admitted to the Equity side of the Court of Exchequer.

Attorneys' certificate books: E109/1–2 with certificates of admission at /3. These only cover the years 1729–1730.

At the **Court of Chancery** and the **Supreme Court of Justice**, indexes of articles and clerkship are in various series:

C216 – this contains the records of solicitors after the Petty Bag Office was formed, making rolls of admission records for solicitors, and this is when the term 'attorney' was dropped. The Petty Bag Office was the main office on the common law side of the court of chancery – all original writs were issued there. Writs had originally been kept in a sack called in Latin a *parva baga*. The Office was abolished when the common law jurisdiction of the Court of Chancery was transferred to the High Court of Justice. The indexes are at C216/21 to 25 and they are on microfilm also. Then the index to affidavits of Due Execution of Articles are at KB170/13 for 1874–1877 and at IND1/29729–29733 for the years 1877–1886. Oath rolls of Catholic solicitors are at C217/180/5 for 1791–1813 and at C214/23/1 for 1838–1867.

There are miscellaneous other admissions to courts, including the palatinates. The **Court of Bankruptcy** admissions registers, for London and for others outside London, are in the series B2/8–11. This is complemented by lists of attorneys who have been admitted in other courts, and the records are in the form of oath rolls and residence books, applications for certificates of admission and certificate books: all these are found at IND 1/4592 and then at KB113, KB169/1 and 2 and then at J89/1 to 10 for certificate applications and at J89/23/1 to 39 for certificate books.

For the **Palatinate of Lancaster** the years 1749–1871 are in various places, but all the main documents will be in the range of PL23/1–6, and for the **Palatinate of Durham** the range is: DURH9/1–3 and at DURH3/218 and 217. The register of certificates to practise for the years 1785 to 1842 are at IND1/10152. For the Palatinate of Chester the materials cover:

Affidavits of Due Execution of Articles of Clerkship, Registers of Addidavits of Due Execution, admission rolls and oath rolls. These are found at CHES36/1 and 36/3 covering the years 1749–1830.

For **ecclesiastical courts**, the term *proctor* was used for their own solicitors, and records of proctors are linked to both the **High Court of Admiralty** and the **Prerogative Court of Canterbury**. A mixture of documents on proctors' work and status are in HCA30 and there are also muniments books for the Admiralty at HCA50. Muniments were title deeds to land, in the general meaning, but here they refer to any document fortifying or making good a claim. For the Canterbury papers of proctors, see PROB29 for the years 1659–1857.

With the Test Act of 1672 and the Corporation Act of 1661, people with official posts again had to take an oath, the former to prove they had taken Holy Communion and the latter to prohibit Catholics and some non-conformists from being elected to local government. To complement this, on the accession of Queen Anne in 1702, the Security of Succession Act was made to force people to reject all support of Jacobite claims to the throne. The oaths were taken publicly in courts; so apart from the oaths mentioned above, there are some of the more broadly national and political found at C214 and in C203.

For all sources on legal professionals, the first step is to consult the research guides, available to read online. There is a listing of all the guides on TNA's site.

Another resource at TNA worth noting are the files in the Home Office records under judges' reports, which are now being comprehensively calendared, and reference should be made to *Ancestors* (monthly magazine), issue 59, for an explanation of this. These are at HO47 and cover the years 1783 –1830. These may contain everything from responses to pleas for pardon or commutation to threatening letters. It is in the statements made in short reports that some interesting biographical material emerges, as in a report made in 1783 by John Rose on a prisoner called White, who had been convicted for stealing lead from a chapel roof: 'I think it would not be consistent with public safety to permit the prisoner to remain here. I see no reason to recommend the prisoner to His Majesty's mercy.'

Finally, at the time of writing this section, the Anglo-American Legal Tradition website is gathering examples from several major series of legal records covering the years between 1200 and 1650, and these will eventually include records from the King's Bench, Common Pleas, Chancery orders and Decrees and memoranda rolls. The website is: www.aalt.law.uh.edu

County Record Offices

Clearly, a search in the Access to Archives facility will bring all kinds of miscellaneous records in listings across the land. The A2A listings of coroners' records are also found at TNA, and there the researcher will find a vast array of materials from coroners' records across many counties. If your ancestor was a coroner, then this would be the speediest way to take a first step in tracing him. For instance, if we take the case of Gloucestershire in the mid-Victorian years, we have this:

𝔖𝔢𝔩𝔡𝔢𝔫 𝔖𝔬𝔠𝔦𝔢𝔱𝔶

SELECT CASES

FROM THE

CORONERS' ROLLS

A.D. 1265–1413

WITH A BRIEF ACCOUNT OF THE

HISTORY OF THE OFFICE OF CORONER

EDITED

FOR THE SELDEN SOCIETY

BY

CHARLES GROSS, Ph.D.

ASSISTANT PROFESSOR OF HISTORY, HARVARD UNIVERSITY

LONDON

BERNARD QUARITCH, 15 PICCADILLY

1896

The Seldon Society's Coroners' Rolls, 1896. Author's collection

Gloucestershire Archives: Records of the Coroner for the Lower Division (CO1/N/1)
The files commence in May 1855 when William Galsford was Deputy Coroner. He became coroner in July, 1855. William Galsford appointed W. Scott as Deputy Coroner during the period 1872–74, and thereafter the filing of inquests, correspondence and notices of date range: 1855–1875.

It may be seen from this that if the researcher knows the approximate dates in office of the ancestor, then the basic information is there online. The records in A2A are mostly process documents, but there are letters, and these will prove to be more useful in filling

Part of a solicitor's report on a licence refusal at Market Rasen. Lincolnshire Archives

out biographical details, as in the papers of George Marris, Deputy Coroner in Lindsey, held at Lincolnshire Archives.

However, it has to be pointed out that the material at County Record Offices which will probably bring most information for the present reasons will be the firm histories. As the case study at the end of this chapter will show, there is a vast amount of information about the daily lives of solicitors here: the documentation is usually in boxes and the range of printed and manuscript material may be vast. The best advice is to start with a search term which is simply the name of the occupation. For example, a search for 'justices' clerks' brings a very long list, and this is typical of the kind of information which will arise – this one opening up a fascinating contextual reference:

D. Allan Crockatt's Magistracy (Leeds Brotherton Library) 7 February 1877, typescript photocopy. Letter to Mr Lewthwaite, Justcies' Clerk's office. Typescript carbon copy. Attached are papers for a meeting of the Officers of the Magistrates' Association . . .

In contrast, if we think of a typical general task of a clerk at quarter sessions, here is an entry from the Michaelmas Quarter Sessions at Dolgellau:

Writ of *venire facias* for GQS at Dolgellau on Friday 10 October 1783. Tested by Sir Watkin Williams Wynne, bart, keeper of the rolls at Dolgellau 5 September 1783. Issued by Anwyl deputy clerk [*venire facias* was a writ to summon a person to appear in court, ordinarily for a petty misdemeanour].

In other words, the materials at County Record Offices are vast and they cover all kinds of aspects of the work done by all categories of legal professionals. The only way to make the search easier is to visit the archives and use the index, searching under the subject catalogue also for additional material. A search under 'solicitor' could bring records of family firms, or records from a number of occasions within the process of the criminal justice system of the past, or from civil affairs at county court and so on.

Newspapers and reports

Naturally, the national and regional newspapers of years gone by are full of court reports and obituaries. Court reports will tell you very little about the legal professional unless the case is high profile, and even then, you may have the words of your ancestor if he or she was a barrister or a judge, but little more. The major court resources, such as the Old Bailey Sessions papers (online) will be packed with verbatim discourse if your ancestor was one of the few who sat in judgement there or who worked as an advocate. But otherwise, obituaries will be the most promising resource. For instance, *The Gentleman's Magazine*, running from the mid eighteenth century to the late nineteenth century, carried obituaries and reports from the provinces on the lives and deaths of eminent persons.

If the approximate dates in office are known, then these kinds of entries will appear in *The Gentleman's Magazine* (these are from the 1806 edition):

Aged 65, Mr Samuel Patch, formerly judge-advocate at Jamaica, but who had for some time resided at Stamford, Co. Lincoln, under the pressure of the most indigent circumstances. He has left an unprotected idiot daughter, whose only inheritance is the poor-house, and the beneficence of her fellow creatures.

Or, here is a more orthodox, very ordinary entry:

At Bath, after only three days illness, R K Hutcheson, barrister at law, son of the late William Hutcheson esq. of Bristol, and a lineal descendant on his mother's side of John Kyrle, esq., of Ross in Herefordshire, the justly celebrated 'Man of Ross'. [The Man of Ross was John Kyrle, a charitable man made famous in a poem by Alexander Pope.]

On the other hand, if the dates are known when the ancestor practised as a magistrate or judge, then the newspaper reports will have some useful complementary information, if only the words spoken are given, or sometimes a comment by a reporter. Obviously, even the smallest report from local magistrates' courts will have some kind of reference to the legal professionals involved. Usually this is as in this example from a case at the West Riding Assizes in 1860: 'At the West Riding Assizes before Mr Justice Cave John Hodgson and William Burke were indicted . . . Mr C Stuart Wortley appeared for the prosecution, Mr Lockwood represented the prisoner Hodgson and Mr Mellor defended Burke.' Those short references may be all the researcher may gather in such cases, but persistence may reap rewards. The simplest approach is to search the name in a

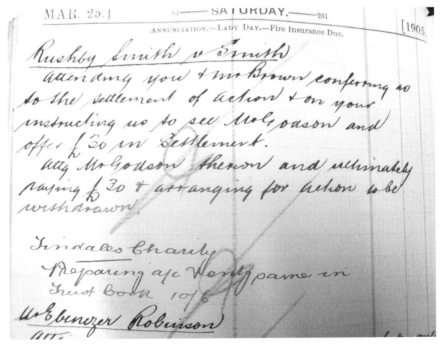

Extract from a solicitor's notebook, 1905. Lincolnshire Archives

circumscribed period and the chances are that some court appearances will demand more details of the barrister involved.

In fact, certainly for the period of the Regency, there are interesting sources for assize trials: many were reported by journalists and writers, and a fruitful exercise is to gather press reports alongside memoirs by judges and barristers and fill out details from the bare bones. Some journalists, for instance Robert Patrick Watson, kept notes on many trials throughout the period c.1860–1880 (see bibliography). Also, there are the law reports from all kinds of sources, and as noticed earlier, these are listed with dates in the *Dictionary of Law* by Mozley and Whiteley.

Parliamentary papers

Parliamentary or sessional papers are produced by both the House of Commons and the House of Lords. There are three categories from the Commons:

Commons
Lords
Command

There are printed indexes for these years:

1696–1834: Catalogue of parliamentary reports
1801–1968/9 General index to the accounts and papers
From 1969 there are the Stationery office catalogues

Online there is access through www.parlipapers.chadwyck.co.uk
The Irish University Press printed the reports and papers for 1800–1899.

In the whole body of parliamentary papers, arguably the most useful for family history research are the materials in several volumes covering legal administration. Here there is a wealth of detail on all aspects of legal work, with information on specific offices and professions. In enquiries and reports there are also massive numbers of materials with minute listings on aspects of

REPORTS

FROM

COMMISSIONERS:

TEN VOLUMES.

—(5.)—·

COMMON LAW;

FIRST REPORT OF HIS MAJESTY'S COMMISSIONERS.

Session

5 February—24 June 1829.

VOL. IX.

Parliamentary Papers: a legal report of 1829. Author's collection individuals who spoke to officials or who gave their name to a list of requests. For example, in a long enquiry into the courts of common law in Wales there are lists of magistrates for Glamorgan in that year, so that we learn, for example, these names and residences:

We, the undersigned magistrates for the County of Glamorgan, not having been present at Swansea at the last general quarter sessions, beg leave to testify by our signatures our cordial concurrence in the above Resolutions:
  T B Rous, Courtyrala
  Thomas Stacy, Gellygaer
  Sir Charles Morgan, bart. Tredegur
  Charles Morgan, Ruperna

Sometimes there are verbatim reports involving lawyers of various kinds, and names appear in the indexes. Thomas Denman, for instance, spoke up concerning the enquiry into the courts system: 'I suggest that the monopoly of serjeants in the Common Pleas be abolished, and the practice of the Exchequer thrown open to all who may desire to be attorneys of that court . . . .' It may be seen how relevant this is to the annotated rules in the preceding section about the admission of provincial lawyers into those superior courts.

Perhaps the most valuable feature of the resources here are the details of the duties and organisation of staff and structures of the various legal institutions. For instance there are scales of fees paid to clerks and administrators for work on documents, and specific legal departments are summarised in terms of the work they do and the staff at work there. This gives a unique insight into the functions that the ancestor may have done in the 'job description' that will be in the census and elsewhere. The references found may well have the word 'clerk' for the occupation, and that could refer to any number of posts, so a dictionary of law will have to be at hand.

In the questions to witnesses one of the most enlightening features is that the reader learns about the various posts and their duties in the legal process, as in this interchange from 1833, when the actions taken by personnel were clarified:

Q   Are there any other proper officers in the Exchequer to carry
     through the decree?
A   No.
Q   Who takes the minute?
A   One of the Masters.
Q   Who draws it up?
A   The Clerk in the Court of the Party.

State Papers

Another useful resource is the State Papers online archive; this
covers state documents from the sixteenth and seventeenth
centuries, and one of the topics included is law and order. A search
with 'Law' brings a very long list of subjects, but within this there
are, for instance, over 2,000 hits for the word 'attorney' and thirty-
five calendar entries for 'Justice of Assize'. A typical entry summary,
with name, is:

> Robert Catlyn, Lord Chief Justice, to Cecil. On the law and
> punishment of witchcraft and sorcery. Allusions to the
> opinions of Henry de Bracton . . . [Bracton was an early legal
> theorist]

Case Study: A family of solicitors

The firm of Peake, Snow and Jeudwine were a typical provincial
firm of solicitors from Sleaford, their beginnings reaching back to the
early nineteenth century. In the national media, their name would
only be acknowledged in the occasional announcements in the
London Gazette when they advertised for claims after a death, as they
acted as executors. Otherwise, their substantial archives, now at the
Lincolnshire Archives, reveal the everyday dealings of the staff, and
if your ancestor was known to have worked for a provincial
company, then you are highly likely to find all kinds of documentation of his career.

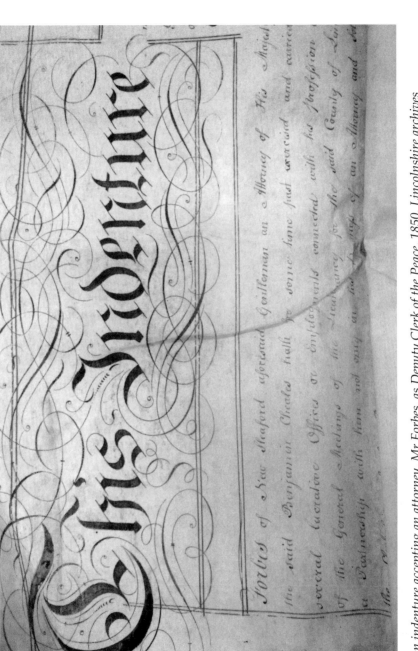

An indenture accepting an attorney, Mr Forbes, as Deputy Clerk of the Peace, 1850. Lincolnshire archives

The archive for this Sleaford firm contains diaries, notebooks, almanacs, letters and a variety of official documents. A list of jobs and payments immediately gives the reader the overall picture of the routine matters such a firm would have dealt with:

December:

Peatmen	search	3 s.
Stephen Thompson	Deed of release	10.s
T R Perl	Land charge	1 s
Grammar School	agreement	10s
S W C Goulding	conveyance	£2 10s

In this particular archive, there is a document from 1850 swearing in Henry Peake as a competent Clerk of the Peace 'for parts of Kesteven in the county of Lincoln' and Mr Moore, who signed the document, signed his name beneath the assertion that Mr Peake was '. . . an able and sufficient person instructed and learned in the laws of England and residing in the said parts to hold and execute the said office of Clerk of the Peace . . .'

Regarding the profile of work done, for the bulk of the years from the mid-nineteenth century to the Edwardian period, there is a considerable volume of work relating to apprenticeship indentures, signed and confirmed, including disciplinary matters, one of which is a sworn statement by an apprentice that he did not annoy a stall-holder in a market place when he should have been at work: 'Dear Sir, Mr Price complained about my misconduct on Monday in the market place. I was going through the market and stopped and had some ice cream and had a word or two with Mrs Brown. I do not remember misconducting myself . . . .'

One solicitor in 1844 kept a diary in a general almanac, and we have plain statements of typical work: 'Engaged this day in going over and certifying book of references in the parishes of Metheringham and Dunstan . . .' and 'Went to Blankney, Lincoln and Metheringham on the business of the Cambridge and Lincoln Railway.'

There were also the usual representations, the more active side of the profession, with records such as 'Attending you and Mr Brown confirming to the settlement of action and on your instructing us to see Mr Godson and offer £30 in settlement . . . '

Overall, this is an immensely important resource for tracing legal ancestors, and there is much more to be done on this in the general area of local and family history.

Chapter Seven
THE LITERATURE OF THE JUDICIARY

Biography

If the researcher is fortunate in having a judge or barrister from the years c.1800–1960, then there is a very high probability that he or she will figure in biographies and of course in obituaries in the newspapers. Often, although the famous figures dominate in this respect, there is a large amount of material available (in the out of print stocks) from all kinds of legal professionals.

The most recently expanded and refined central resource for the lives of legal professionals is *The Oxford Dictionary of National Biography* (ODNB); until recent years, it was only possible to find entries on celebrated figures such as Lord Chancellors and high-profile judges. But now its website features a biographical essay, *Lives of the Law* and this presents a survey of all main categories of lives connected in some way to English law. The introduction on the site hints at the new developments: 'Of its 55,000 biographies of men, women, and (on rare occasions) children from British history, well over half of them newly written, the remainder revised and edited, a substantial proportion relate . . . to the law.' The aim is now, therefore, to present the reader with a comprehensive resource on all aspects of workers in and about the law over the centuries. Many of these people in the entries are not well known generally. The entries include:

Judicial authors and lawmakers

This has cross-references to influential writers and theorists such as Sir John Fortescue, Sir Thomas Littleton and Sir Edward Coke. There

Montagu Williams, barrister and memorist. Author's collection

are also entries on major figures who had an impact on major areas of legal work.

Advocates

Of course, most of these entries are on influential figures such as Sir Edward Marshall Hall and Thomas Erskine, but the essay points out that 'The *Dictionary* also celebrates the achievements of another and less transient nature – such as that of Ivy Williams (1877–1966) the first woman called to the English Bar . . . She enjoyed a very distinguished academic career, but did not practise.' The first woman who did practise law, Helena Normanton, is of course, in the *Dictionary*.

Solicitors

As the essay on the site notes, 'In the original dictionary solicitors were greatly under-represented, no doubt reflecting the reticence of a profession that does good by stealth . . . ' But now the *Dictionary* includes the results of the work done by Judy Slinn, for instance, as noted in chapter 6, on the Freshfield family of solicitors, which provides an exemplary family history in miniature, the entry being written by Slinn herself. Also included are Sir William Slaughter and William May, for example, who formed their own partnership in 1889, and whose life again presents a template for family biography.

Ecclesiastical and canon lawyers

These legal professionals were not included in the original ODNB but now there are listings and entries for a number of influential figures such as Dr Walter Catchpol, Thomas Oughton and Francis Topham. One mysterious entry is for Peter Dene, whose face is depicted in one of the windows at York Minster, and who was called by one writer 'a dreadful snake'. As for Topham, he appears in transmuted fictional form in the classic novel by Laurence Sterne, *Tristram Shandy*.

The most potentially helpful sources are going to be in County Record Offices and in university and cathedral libraries. For instance, at the University of Durham, in the Special Collections, there are court records and court proctors' papers. There is a hand list of proctor's papers for individual consistory court causes (the Bishop's court). These are at GB-0033 and at A66–69 from the site of the University: www.dur.ac.uk/library

Judge Henry Hawkins, later Lord Brampton. Author's collection

The judiciary

Naturally, judges figure prominently in the entries. But the guide points out that 'The new dictionary of course includes biographies of many judges, ranging from the stars of the legal firmament, through the important ranks of able and conscientious judicial journeymen, to others of less flattering reputation.' There is such a large number of entries under this category that some researchers will most likely discover a family connection: some are discoveries, in the sense that they are figures in the law who need to be more widely known, such as Jonathan Christian (1808–1887) who was a leader of the Irish Equity Bar and who became a judge of the Irish Court of Common Pleas. Over the years there has been a very large number of such office-holders.

Law reporters

At the heart of the systems of legal procedures in all contexts, there has been the skill of law reporting, going back to early Middle Ages, and some of the first and also the most famous of these reporters are in the dictionary. These include Sir Roger Townshend, Sir Richard Pollard, and John Caryll, who was 'one of the first identifiable law reporters'. Important figures in more recent times are William Best and GJP Smith, who both had no time for the official boy of their profession, the Council of Law Reporting, as they considered it to be a threat to their independence. The Incorporated Council for Law Reporting, founded in 1865, has the objective of the 'preparation and publication, in a convenient form, at a moderate price, and under gratuitous professional control, of reports of judicial decisions of the Superior and Appellate courts of England and Wales.' Their office is in Chancery Lane, close to the Law Society.

Overall, then, the ODNB provides a massive resource of family history, and in terms of firm histories for instance, or of biographies which open out some understanding of what the legal profession was like at a particular time, it is uniquely valuable.

Of course, there is also the publication, *Who's Who*. This biographical dictionary has been in print since 1893, and it is in here that you are likely to find the kind of legal professional who made his or her mark in any one of a number of ways, such as the example of James Beresford Atlay, who was born in Leeds in 1860, and won an open scholarship to Oriel College, Oxford where he studied History. He was called to the Bar at Lincoln's Inn in 1887, and he later became a specialist commissioner for income tax. But where he distinguished himself was in his writing about law, as in his books, *The Trial of Lord Cochrane* (1897) and his editorship of Hall's *International Law* in 1904 and 1909.

Memoirs

There is a huge resource for family historians in the literature of legal memoirs. They are often out of print but not so difficult to find by inter-library loan; and many are inexpensive to buy from specialist second-hand dealers. The topic here is about memoirs in various categories, some more useful than others:

* Memoirs of the celebrated figures in law such as judges and barristers
* Autobiographies printed locally or by specialist presses
* Works by professionals on routine law eg magistrates' lives

A typical example of the most useful is the kind of Victorian or Edwardian publication which is indexed and which includes cases, information on the legal process and of course, accounts of the social and professional context of their world. A typical example of this is *Some Experiences of a Barrister's Life* by Mr Serjeant Ballantine. This was published in 1883 and has chapter summaries included in the contents pages. The value of this kind of memoir is that it contains accounts of what the professional life of a barrister was in the mid-nineteenth century at the Inns of Court. But there are also several names given, people in his circle and with whom he conducted legal business or socialised. For instance, in one chapter he writes about the 'choice of circuit' and in that he mentions eighteen other barristers of the period, and notes the circuits their work entailed.

To this must be added the volumes on true crime biography which include plenty of biography from the broader context, and these works are usually written by specialists in true crime and criminology. A template example of this, with a very special value for research, is Richard Whittington-Egan's *William Roughead's Chronicles of Murder* (1991). This has a long and detailed fact file on all kinds of legal biographies from the period c.1900–1950, covering judges, barristers, scholars of the law, historians of law and professionals who were involved in writing about the legal situation and issues of their time.

Memoirs of judges and barristers enjoyed a boom period in the Edwardian years and in the 1890s to a certain extent. It was in that time that the new publishers on the scene took an interest in trials and the process of law. On the more educational side, we have books such as Edward Manson's *Builders of Our Law During the Reign of Queen Victoria*, which includes thirty-five biographies of judges; or the typical *Famous Judges and Famous Trials* by Charles Kingston, which again deals with the lives and cases of judges, covering twelve men. It was in this period that there were a number of books on lawyers and trials with the word 'romance' in the title – a strange fact, hinting that court dramas and barristers' lives were becoming popular narratives with a compelling fascination rather different from previous Newgate tales. Examples were *Notable Trials: Romances of the Law Courts* by R Storry Deans, and *Romances of the Forum* by Peter Burke.

However, memoirs are in print by people who were part of the law machinery at the bench, such as *This Old Wig* by JB Sandbach, which contains ' . . . some recollections of a former London Metropolitan Police magistrate (1944)'. This gives an account of the work done at Marlborough Street court, which Sandbach tells us was once 'originally the town house of one of the Regency bucks . . . ' But today it is an hotel, just around the corner from the London Palladium, having film stars as guests, treading the floor where once Oscar Wilde came to attend court.

The value of these kinds of publications is that they give a unique insight into the legal context in which the various occupations would have been active, from the usher to the clerk and the bench.

Obituaries

Clearly, the obituaries in national and local newspapers are of real value for the present subject. With local and regional papers, there may not be an index for any period but the most recent few years. But as long as the researcher knows the time period the ancestor was working, then a sweep of the national papers may well bring up the obituary, with some persistence.

In a sample search, looking at the first six months of the year 1890, there were twenty-five members of the legal profession in *The Times* obituaries, and the contrasts are basically these:

A substantial biographical summary of prominent figures, such as Baron Dowse, who died in March of that year. Dowse died while he was on circuit and had charged the grand jury just the day before his death. These entries give notes and insights into personality, such as, 'He gave at all times free and vivid utterance to his thoughts without waiting to examine critically the terms in which he moulded them.'

Brief summary of administrators and typically busy law people, as this for William Joseph Foster in June of that year:

Mr Foster was a solicitor by profession, having been admitted in 1869. He was elected a member of the Common Council for Cornhill Ward in 1886 and he showed such an aptitude for municipal work that he was chosen as chairmen of the committee [The Law and City Courts Committee].

Most common is the entry in a multiple obituary such as this:

We have to announce the death . . . of Mr Charles Crompton QC, bencher of the Inner Temple . . . He was placed fourth wrangler in 1855 and was afterwards elected fellow of his college. [Wranglers at Cambridge was the term for the order in the subject honours list.]

Case study: More listings in specialist publications

Legal historians have provided family historians with a variety of specific sources, and these refer to occupations or to admissions to certain Inns or professional status. These are some examples.

Admissions to Clement's Inn

This list is in print, from the Selden Society, edited by Sir John Sainty. The list was taken from a source at TNA, and the entries are arranged by term: namely Hilary, Easter, Trinity and Michaelmas. The editor wrote to county archivists for information as well, and the clerk dealing with the admissions added information where that was available. This gives us this kind of entry, with 'g' meaning 'gentleman' and the attached name being the name of the person's surety:

> 1709
> William Atkinson, Spalding, Lincs. G. – Maurice Johnson
> William Barnes, Whitborne, Heref. G. – James Smith
> 1710
> Samuel Eccles, Tiddeswall, Derbs. G. – Charles Bagshaw

Then the clerk's notes are in footnotes, so that we have this for Eccles: 'Eccles married a daughter of Thomas Statham, a half-sister of Sir John Statham and was thus connected with Bagshaw, his surety.'

Holders of Patents of Precedence

This refers to the practice in which the Crown gave permission and licence to practise, but originally not under the Great Seal. Other types of a typical admission to practise applied here also. The years in this Selden publication cover 1687–1897, and the details are minimal but useful, as in this:

> DAUNCEY, PHILIP
> Gt. of precedence after KC 19 April
> D. 14 June, 1819 (*Gentleman's Magazine*, 1819)

Lawyers practising in Chancery, 1474–1486

The eminent legal historian, JH Baker, has done a massive amount of work on legal biographies, and this article from *The Journal of Legal History* exemplifies the kind of specific source that will be a real gift to a researcher who is in need of more reference in Medieval or Early Modern law offices. Baker's task was that he had to use bills in Chancery, and these had the names of two pledges of prosecution. He adds, ' . . . the names were clearly the names of real people . . . What is remarkable is that about one third of them are described as being "of London, gentleman"'. A quarter of his samples were attorneys of the common law courts.

Local resources – off-beat

One legal professional who has not been mentioned so far is the sheriff. This position represents the principal crown office in a county; the post entails, among other things, supervision of elections and making sure the process of law in the courts is done according to procedure. The origin of the word is in 'shire reeve' and the office may be traced back as far as the reign of Ethelred the Unready (978–1016). In the medieval period the job involved a great diversity of tasks, including proclaiming statutes and collecting land revenue.

An example of a more unusual and very welcome source is that of a sheriff's notebook from the fifteenth century found in the Darell papers. George Darell was sheriff of Wiltshire in 1464–1465 and in his notes there are details of payments made to him for expenses. The scholar who worked on this notes: 'This small book, of which eight and a half folios are written or partly written, and the remainders are blank, contains days of the sittings of the county court, presided over by the sheriff; the names of officials with whom he had to deal; royal and county officials such as the justices of the peace and the coroners; private officials such as the bailiffs . . . '

Basically, there is a huge amount of biographical material for all kinds of legal offices over the centuries, but they are in mostly obscure places. The best place to start, as always, is in a search at Access to Archives (A2A).

Calendar of Assize Records

Available in print is a calendar of the assize records for the Home Circuit published by HMSO. There are ten volumes, all drawn from the indictment files and the nature of these records is varied and indeed unpredictable. But most valuable for family historians are the lists of assize judges. For instance, all the Home Circuit judges for the years 1559–1625 are here, in this form:

> Altham, James B 1607 W
> Carus, Thomas, serjeant 1559 W
> Chamberlain, Thomas J 1624W–1624S
> [W – also acted on Western Circuit]

Poll Books

In an Act of Parliament of 1696 poll books were authorised, and they were published up to the year 1871, issued after elections if there was a demand. Names and occupations will generally be found here, so clearly this is a good starting point or a point of reference. After the 1872 Secret Ballots Act, they were abolished. They are basically listings of the classes which owned property, and so lawyers will clearly be listed.

The National Library of Wales

There are some outstandingly useful collections in this library in Aberystwyth. The main categories are in companies and individual collections, papers of judges and county records. For example, a typical summary of a deposit is:

> GB0210 FRAGREEN
> Deeds and personal papers acquired by Francis Green, 13th Century – 1923 including deeds and papers relating to Pembrokeshire and to the Green family 1806–1880; records of the office of James Summers, solicitor

𝕷𝖆𝖜 𝕹𝖔𝖙𝖊𝖘

A

MONTHLY MAGAZINE

FOR

PRACTITIONERS AND STUDENTS

VOL. LXVII.

LONDON:

"LAW NOTES" PUBLISHING OFFICES, 25 & 26, CHANCERY LANE.

1948

Frontispiece for Law Notes, *1948. Author's collection*

On a larger scale, there is a massive source for the Henry Rumsey Williams papers (GB0210), covering 'draft conveyances, abstracts of title, letters, accounts and miscellaneous papers of clients . . . '

This is an immense resource for legal professionals working in Wales over the centuries.

Chapter Eight
THE SERVANTS TO THE LAW MACHINE

Other professionals: ancillary groups

If reference is made to the *Law List*, then the sheer number and diversity of legal professionals is easily grasped. This chapter provides a survey of some of these other professions, partly to explain what they were and what the post-holders did, and partly to see what sources there are for these people's lives. As it is impossible to go through every occupation exhaustively, these are in groups under generic names.

Clerks

The House of Commons and the House of Lords have their clerks, and in the Court of Chancery there is a Clerk of the Crown. At the more diurnal, mundane level there is the justice's clerk and also the barrister's clerk. Therefore the word is applied sometimes for very high-level administrative work, traditionally the person who would issue writs, and in inferior courts throughout the land the clerk, in a more straightforward organisational sense, would do a multiplicity of work.

In the Chancery, the Clerk of the Crown issued writs for elections, and certified the election of peers. But at the local and regional courts, the justice's clerk is the assistant to the justice. Formerly it was the practice that the justice would educate a person as their secretary. But over time, the clerk became an officer of the court with an advisory task, as he had to know the law and advise magistrates who, however well experienced in some matters, needed guidance on legal principles.

Know all Men by these Presents
that I Maurice
Peter Moore of New Sleaford in the County of Lincoln
Gentleman Clerk of the peace for the parts of Kesteven
in the said County do by these presents nominate elect
appoint and assign *Henry Peake* of new
Sleaford in the C of Lincoln Gentleman an able
and sufficient person instructed and learned in the
Laws of England and residing in the said parts
and County to be my Deputy Clerk of the peace for the
said parts To hold and execute the said office of
Deputy Clerk of the peace for the parts aforesaid and to
exercise use and enjoy all such powers and authorities
belonging or incident To my said office as fully and
effectually to all intents and purposes as I myself might
or could do if I were personally present and did the
same In Witness whereof I have hereunto set my hand
and seal this   day of   in the year
of our Lord one thousand eight hundred and fifty

Maurice Peter Moore
Clerk of the Peace

Henry Peake is accepted as Deputy Clerk of the Peace, 1850. Lincolnshire Archives

Barristers' clerks are quite another matter. Serjeant Ballantine had this to say on the topic back in c.1840: 'A mischievous little urchin cleaned my boots, and was called clerk.' But of course, there is much more to it than that. In 1936 a feature in *The Times* pointed out the real status of this clerk:

The idea that a barrister's clerk was once a dingy, Dickensian figure in a dingy room, merely existing to take a brief, boil his master's kettle for tea, and shield him from the sordid work of collecting fees, is derived rather from fancy than from fact . . . The increasing importance and prosperity of some barristers' clerks is therefore not particularly revolutionary nor necessarily undesirable . . .

The basic definition of the profession is that the clerk manages and administrates the barristers' chambers. The job is regulated by the Institute of Barristers' Clerks, which was formed in 1922. The clerk has to know the barristers they work with and they have to manage a diary, look after the chambers, and know the nature of the specific branch of law dealt with in their chambers.

Possibly the most vivid description of the office is this from Montagu Williams QC, from his autobiography, *Later Leaves* (see bibliography):

A type of character only to be met with in the Temple and its precincts is the barrister's clerk. He usually begins life as chambers boy, his business in that capacity being to make himself generally useful, and when the clerk is in court with his master, to see anyone who calls, and note down in a book the object of the visit.

When they first formed their association in 1922, they were noticed and commented on as they tended to appear in court. One legal correspondent described them like this: 'They are not solicitors' clerks; they have not the self-conscious look of wonderment common to law students and waiting witnesses, nor the apprehensiveness of "parties". Their faces bear the imprint of the law. They are, in fact,

BRECONSHIRE, To Wit.

A TABLE of FEES, to be taken by Justices' Clerks, and Constables, under the Statute of the 5th and 6th Victoria, cap. 109, intituled, "An Act for the appointment and payment of Parish Constables," as settled by the Justices assembled at the General Quarter Sessions of the Peace, held in and for the said County, the 2nd day of January, 1843, and approved of by Her Majesty's principal Secretary of State for the Home Department, on the 9th day of January, 1843.

Justices' Clerks' Fees.

	s.	d.
For every Precept to High Constable for convening a Special Petty Sessions, to be paid by each Parish	1	0
Notices to Justices, when required, to be paid by each Parish	0	6
Precept and Notice to Overseers, to return Lists to Special Sessions, including abstract of duties, to be paid by each Parish	1	0
Each Form of List of Persons agreed to at Vestry, when required by Overseer	0	3
For every other Precept and Notice issued under this Act	1	6
Verification and allowance of each List returned, including hearing objections thereto	1	6
Appointment of Constable, if only one, including Oath	2	0
Each additional Constable, in the same appointment	0	6
Copy of appointment for Overseers, one half.		
Every Summons and Duplicate	1	6
List of Constables for Justices and Clerk of the Peace, each Parish	1	0
For every order of Justices, to unite Parishes, under Section 4, to be paid by each Parish, included therein	1	0
For every Copy	0	6
For every information and examination, if in writing	2	0
For each witness examined on hearing, including Oath	1	0
Conviction, where no form is prescribed	2	6
Distress Warrant	2	0
Commitment	2	0
Other orders and allowances not provided for	1	6

Constables' Fees.

	s.	d.
Serving Summons within the Parish	1	0
Executing Warrant	2	6
Distraining, when not otherwise directed by Statute	2	6
Pressing Carriages for baggages, each	1	0
For assistance in making a return, or obeying a legal order of Justices	2	0
For attendance with Prisoner	2	6
For assistance with Prisoner when necessary	2	6
Travelling expenses per mile, (both ways,) when out of the Parish	0	3
For taking a Prisoner into Custody, or before a Justice, per mile	0	3
Subsistence of Prisoner, per day,	0	9
Subsistence of Constable, after one day	2	0
Assistant, when ordered, same as Constable.		
Lodging of Prisoner.	0	9
Lodging of Constable	2	0
Assistant to Constable	2	0
For the performance of such other occasional duties, which may be required of the said Constables, under a written order of Justice, not exceeding 2s. 6d. per Day, and 3s. per Night.		

POWELL,

Clerk of the Peace.

Breconshire justices, 1843. Welsh Legal History Society

barristers' clerks.' Obviously, this denigrates as well as pays tribute, and surely it belittles the occupation, pandering to a Dickensian view of the clerk in general. Barristers' memoirs do tend to have a tinge of arrogance and a love of the telling anecdote or exaggeration.

For justices' clerks, we may also learn something of their work and fees from court records, as in this list from Breconshire in 1843, a table of fees:

Justices' Clerks' Fees	s.	p.
For every precept to High Constable for convening a Special Petty Sessions, To be paid by each parish	1	0
Notices to justices, when required, to be paid to each parish		6
Precept and Notice to Overseers, to return lists to Special Sessions, Including abstracts of duties, to be paid by each parish	1	0

The clerk was also paid a shilling for producing summonses, examining witnesses, issuing a distress warrant, writing a form for commitment and for making the agreement for the appointment of a constable. Note: a *precept* was an official order.

Administrators

In the various processes and institutions related to civil litigation, there will be a number of professions to consider. As Amanda Bevan points out in her guide to the records at TNA, the related records make up a very large and under-used part of the holdings there. These records are basically about disputes, mostly about land and possessions, rights and so on. Searching for legal ancestors here is a secondary task, to fill out details of the life and activities of the ancestor, because using these records is very difficult. The main barrier is the vocabulary of the law: something extremely challenging for the layperson of course.

But at the heart of all the supporting work in a law firm and else-where there is the **legal secretary.** This office is an important part of the team around the firm; Natasha Lawrence explained the work in this way: 'Most of the work the legal secretary handles is paperwork, but depending on the type of case, she/he understands the importance of proper legal procedure, obtaining relevant information, documentation preparation, filing dates, follow-through, court hearings and other necessary steps pertinent to a particular case.'

There have been legal secretaries since the beginning of literature, because there has always been a demand for official records, and as time has gone on, their duties have expanded.

Legal secretaries for ecclesiastical courts have always been important figures, as may be seen for instance in a report on the Bishop of Worcester's appointments in 1905, when he made Messrs Day, solicitors in Westminster, to be his legal secretaries, and a certain Mr J Hooper to be his diocesan legal secretary. In 1950, the Bishop of London appointed Mr Heath and Mr Dashwood as his legal secretaries.

The **registrar** was originally the person who kept the records at the Court of Chancery; he also wrote orders. Now there are registrars of the family division of the county court and also district registrars of the High Court. By the Courts and Legal Services Act of 1990 the registrar today hears and determines some interim assemblies and some final hearings, so the position is akin to that of the traditional judge.

In past times, the registrar was a key administrator in all kinds of places. In the Court of Chancery in 1853, for instance, the formulation of decrees and orders was his responsibility, and delays caused irritation. This letter to *The Times* in that year from 'A London solicitor' expresses the concern. The writer says:

You are aware that decrees and orders of the Court of Chancery are drawn up by the registrar of the court, and in drawing up decrees and orders which deal with a fund in court, the registrar requires a certificate from the Accountant-General of the Court of Chancery . . . Hitherto it has been the practice to deliver that certificate to the solicitor applying . . . on the second day after his bespeaking it. Last Saturday I was greatly surprised on being told by a clerk that it would not be ready until the next Saturday . . .

In other words, the constant changes in procedure – what Hamlet called 'the Law's delay' – always impinge on the administrator's duties, and so they affect lawyers too. One great responsibility they had, along with other administrators, was to draw up reports and accounts. In the mid-Victorian period for instance, these were summarised in the papers as well as figuring in Parliamentary Reports. In 1853, for example, the fees received in the Court of Chancery Registrar's Office totalled £13,334, and in the Examiner's Office it was £700.2s.6d.

Scriveners have always been the legal professionals in the business of controlling and regulating the creation of all kinds of legal documents. The earlier discussion of notaries provides a useful cross-reference here, because notaries are recorded as being members of the Company of Scriveners from the year 1392. The Scriveners were one of the livery companies, and these were organisations of crafts. New ordinances were issued in 1392 at the time when the new Archbishop of Canterbury was appointed as a papal legate.

The Worshipful Company of Scriveners goes back to the time when there were attempts to regulate conveyances – particularly of property, and in 1498 there was another formulation of ordinances, mainly to ensure that apprentices were tested by the wardens. Then, from 1558, members of the Company were forced by the Crown to provide money to help deal with the costs of the war with France. Account books from that time and earlier are held in the Guildhall Library manuscripts collection; these show that cash was paid to the Company by the Freemen of London and by the livery companies.

In 1617 a charter of incorporation was issued to the 'Master, Wardens and Assistants of the Society of Scriveners of London' and in 1634 the Company was given a grant of arms, making the arms which had been in use since early Tudor times official. In 1628 it had its base at Bacon Hall, near Oat Lane in Aldersgate. This was destroyed in the 1666 fire and then was rebuilt and was being used again by 1671. Their most famous Master was perhaps Robert Clayton, who was Lord Mayor in 1680.

Of particular interest is the admittance of women into the profession – something recorded from 1665 and also at that time it was recorded that 'Attornies in the Courts of Law and Solicitors in the

Courts of Equity . . . have taken upon them to exercise the proper art or mystery of Scriveners . . . within the limits and jurisdiction of the Company's charter . . . ' In the seventeenth century scriveners were primarily concerned with land conveyancing and also dealing with loans, and a certain level of competition arose between scriveners and attorneys, and an Act of 1729 was passed to regulate these occupations and specialisms. Reinforcement of this was obtained with the 1801 Public Notaries Act which made all applicants wanting to apply for status of notaries become members of the Company. This of course provided professional gate-keeping on applicants, to make sure that quality of work was maintained.

The oath of the Company of Scriveners includes these words: 'I shall not write, nor suffer to be written by any of mine, to my power or knowledge, any deed or writing to be conceived or in my conscience suspected to lie, nor any deed bearing date of long time past before the ensealing thereof, nor bearing any date of any time to come . . . ' In other words, there has always been a strict professional code of ethics. Today, the Scriveners' Qualification Rules of 1998 govern entry. To qualify as a scrivener, a person has first to qualify as a general notary and then they start a training agreement, followed by an examination.

It is not so hard to find records of scriveners, and the best source is found at British History Online. This has extensive lists, including, for instance, Rawlinson Ms D 51 which has 'Subscriptions to oath and notes on assistants 1628–78,' along with plenty of other sources with names of professionals listed on the site online, for instance:

List of assistants, 1554–5 and those admitted, 1562–3

And

Assistants taken in 1575, 1580–1, 1587

And even named ones such as 'submission of John Valentyne, April, 1446' (see the bibliography for details).

Some of the most well-known scriveners have come to us after research, such as the discovery in 2009 of the identity of the man who was always simply known as Adam the Scrivener, and who worked with Geoffrey Chaucer was unknown, but now we know he was Adam Pinkhurst, the son of a landowner in Surrey, thanks to research by Professor Linne Mooney of Maine, USA. Adam, who worked on Chaucer's manuscripts, earned the wrath of the great poet, who wrote: 'So oft a day I must they work renew/it to correct and also to rub and scrape/ and all is through thy negligence and haste . . . ' Adam's entry is in fact the eighth earliest entry in the members' book of regulations of 1392. As a great help to all family historians, Professor Mooney has complied a list of over 200 scribes who were working in England in the years 1375–1425.

The **examiner** is a person appointed by the Lord Chancellor to record the examination of a witness under action; in addition, a Special Examiner may be appointed to work abroad, examining a witness in a foreign country. An examination of a prisoner in the inquiry regarding the charge against him or her, preparatory to being committed, is the most common application of the term, and a bankrupt may be examined, but these are not related to the post of examiner.

Vestry Clerk

The vestries were traditionally the governing organisations of the parish; the brief was to handle all local issues, whether ecclesiastical or civil, and the vestry clerk was the person who recorded the minutes and administrated affairs. A notable example was Mr Chambers Leete, who became Town Clerk of the Borough of Kensington in 1900, after serving as vestry clerk in 1889. The position became a salaried one by the middle years of the eighteenth century, and under legislation on local government in 1855, the vestry clerk became the main official responsible for organisation and administration. It is plain to see the similarity between these gatherings and ecclesiastical courts, and the duties of the clerks are very similar in both cases.

Since 1980, Chambers have published guides to **legal executives**, listing the people involved and giving profiles of firms. There are (in 2009) 22,000 qualified and trainee legal executives, and that post is recognised as a route towards becoming a lawyer. The Institute of Legal Executives (ILEX) exists as a forum for the profession.

Women working in the law

The placing of this section has little to do with the importance of this aspect of the subject. The fact is that through the centuries, the legal profession was something from which women were excluded. Despite the fact that there was a clause in the Solicitors' Act of 1843 which stated that 'Every word importing the masculine gender only shall extend and be applied to a female as well as to a male' it was not until the Sex Disqualification (Removal) Act of 1919 that all professions had to admit women. But there were women law students at Oxford and Cambridge in the nineteenth century: there was also the option for women to study for an external degree of LL.B. Research by Rosemary Auchmuty has shown that there were no women law students at provincial universities in the Victorian years.

At Cambridge, Janet Wood studied at Girton (1875–1878); Anne Tuthill was also at that college (1876–1879) and Sarah Ellen Mason was there (1878–1881). Girton College opened in 1869, founded by Emily Davies, with just five students. The famous Tripos examination was closed to women until 1991, and there was a Law Tripos, covering nine areas of legal study. There were therefore law students who were women up to the twentieth century, but no practising female lawyers: this came in 1920 when Helena Normanton was called to the Bar and then given brief at the High Court of Justice and the Central Criminal Court in 1922. The first woman solicitor was Carrie Morrison, also a graduate of Girton, who was also admitted in 1922.

Earlier, Margaret Hall had tried to gain admission to the Bar, and in 1903 Bertha Cave applied to study at Gray's Inn. The benchers turned her down. Lord Halsbury said, 'There is no precedent for ladies being called to the English Bar.' There were appeals against these blocks to admission, but progress was slow. Arguably, as in so many occupations, it took the Great War and women's participation in all kinds of new work to change matters.

Undoubtedly the most celebrated woman lawyer of the twentieth century was Dame Rose Heilbron. She died in December, 2005, at the age of 91, and she had been the first women to win a scholarship to Gray's Inn. She was also the first woman to be appointed silk and to take part in a murder case. Her career was a series of legal 'firsts' – including being the first woman recorder and the first female treasurer at Gray's Inn. By 1946 she had appeared in ten murder trials, and when she was just 34, along with Helena Normanton, Heilbron became a King's Counsel. Perhaps her grandest moment was in 1951 when she appeared at the Old Bailey speaking for the Liverpool dockers, defending them against the charge of incitement to strike. The case was withdrawn before it went to the jury. She certainly became famous and respected in Liverpool after that: she was born in that city, to a Jewish family, and her father owned a lodging house for refugees there.

Jack Spot Comer, the gangster, called Heilbron 'the greatest lawyer in history' and told the reporters who had come to write about him to turn their attention to her.

Case study: Ernest Pettifer, Clerk to the Justices

Actual first-hand information and reflections on a justices' clerk and his work are rare in print, but they do exist, and one such publication is *The Court is Sitting* by EW Pettifer (see bibliography).

Pettifer wrote an in-depth account of his profession there, calling the chapter 'The Clerk at Work'. The account of his work is anecdotal but also deeply reflective. Pettifer has many things to say on the nature of his work, but this point made explains the essential demand on him: 'The justices deal with so many matters which are quite distinct from crime that the Clerk must have a working knowledge of the law governing such diverse questions as the adoption of a child, the grant of a medicated wines licence to a chemist or the issue of a certificate to a money-lender.'

In 1940, when Pettifer wrote, the qualifications for the Clerk were that he had to be either a solicitor or a barrister of fourteen years standing. But as he pointed out at the time, 'The solicitor's examinations have very little bearing upon the particular work a Clerk is called upon to handle . . . The trouble has been that no examination has ever been instituted for assistants.' Clerks were then sometimes part-time workers, and again Pettifer had strong opinions on the matter: 'Whole-time Clerks . . . are necessary in all districts save the very small divisions, in thinly-populated areas, where it might be difficult to amalgamate sufficient of the existing courts to form an area sufficiently large enough, and to offer a salary adequate.'

The real importance of the clerk's work may be seen if reference is made to the Local Government Act of 1888, because that made it possible for the chairmen of Urban and Rural Councils to sit as justices on the bench. Clearly, such people needed advice and direction from someone knowledgeable in the law. In addition to the advice and the legal knowledge, Mr Pettifer needed skill in organisation, administration and in using common sense, such as arranging sittings across the week, splitting them equally. He noted that in his own court, three separate cases sat simultaneously, and he had to use his judgement if he thought that a serious case was likely to take a full day, and to allow for that.

In the course of his long career, Mr Pettifer saw children's courts, serious crime, gangland activities, poaching in mining communities during hard times, marital violence cases and many kinds of non-judicial business.

Chapter Nine
LAWYER ANCESTORS IN SCOTLAND
AND IRELAND

The Scottish legal system

The very nature of law creates a vocabulary of its own, and historical research into legal history entails having to deal with not only the obscure and difficult vocabulary itself, but also the complex syntax and level of abstraction. This is particularly true of Scottish law, which has a varied and extensive number of official occupations as well as concepts. Gone are the days when amateurs and enthusiasts such as Dr Johnson could dabble in the concepts, as he did when in Edinburgh:

> Johnson had before this dictated to me a law paper upon a question purely in the law of Scotland, concerning **vicious intromission**, that is to say, meddling with the effects of a deceased person, without a regular title; which formerly was understood to subject the meddler to payments of all the defunct's debts.

There is a need to understand the organisation of Scots law and the offices within the profession, so that family history researchers may have some help through the labyrinth of institutions and functions. For a layperson like Johnson to try to write a learned paper on some element of the law in this context would surely be unthinkable now.

There is no other legal system like the Scottish one; it has its origins in Roman law and has several elements from common law and other sources brought together. With the 1707 union with England there was some element of influence from the English system, but it is only really in commercial law that there is a close similarity between the two codifications. Perhaps the one outstanding difference in the criminal law is the verdict in a Scottish trial of 'not proven'.

There is a Ministry for Justice at the head of the system, and the two main categories of lawyers in Scotland are advocates and solicitors. John Finlay, in an article in the *Edinburgh Law Review*, argues that the basic division in Scotland was not really who was an advocate and who was a solicitor, but who belonged to the College of Justice and who did not (see bibliography for details).

Advocates

The Faculty of Advocates governs the profession, and the term is equivalent to the English barrister: there is a senior and junior counsel. Advocates work in the higher courts, and specialise in presenting cases, after instructions from solicitors. Advocates have to accept the clients who approach, rather than selecting cases, as in England.

Solicitors

The Law Society of Scotland regulates solicitors, who present cases to court; only since 1992 have they had the right to apply for rights to work in the higher courts. Unlike in England, a solicitor may also work as a notary public, after due application and process. Recently this dual classification has coalesced to a degree: since 1990 it has been possible, after examination, for solicitors to apply for work formerly only done by advocates.

The historical reasons for the divergence from the English legal system in Scotland stem from very early times, when in the early medieval centuries Norse and Celtic elements fused, the Norse being termed 'Udal law'. But after the Norman Conquest, and until the independence of Scotland from Norman influence in 1328 there was clearly a system in flux, but from that time matters brought about a consolidation, and courts called burgh courts emerged, being courts similar in level and function to quarter sessions in England. The Dean of Guild Courts then were instituted, handling what would be in England civil law. Above and beyond, at the centre of legislation, a formation of statute law was achieved by c.1300.

As David Moody has written, in his book on family history, 'Given the nature of lawyers' business, there is a high survival rate for their records – many papers are deposited in the gifts and deposits sections of record offices, and many solicitors' offices. If one could obtain access, these are treasure houses, illustrative of the history of the profession' (*Scottish Family History* pp. 46–47). That is exactly right: the sources are scattered but substantial, and the way into them is from the broader sources first, then down to the particular ones.

There have been legal societies, attached to both the inferior and the local courts in Scotland, and these were parallel to the societies known as the Faculty of Advocates and the Society of Writers to the Signet. The so-called country practitioners formed societies to take care of their regulations, and therefore they controlled admissions. Any records of such societies of procurators will of course be valuable sources in family history.

As the English universities doing law courses were closed to Scots until the mid-nineteenth century (because of the 39 Articles of the Church of England being a requisite subscription for candidates), Scots lawyers studied abroad, and hence the influence of Roman law, which existed in parts of Europe. In 1532, a College of Justice was established and two courts, the Scottish Court of Exchequer and the Commissary Courts, were created in that century also. Then, with the Act of Union in 1701, the Scottish system was retained and in the eighteenth century, as the great age of the Enlightenment developed, with Scotland as a key, integral part of that flowering of learning and philosophy, higher education accelerated, and the study of law became an important part of Scottish culture. Many lawyers (like James Boswell and Sir Walter Scott) clearly had as a necessary part of their education a broader cultural awareness and reverence for fraternities of professional men.

If your ancestor was a Scottish lawyer in the eighteenth century and Regency period, then the chances are that he was well educated, a lively social mixer and interested in all kinds of knowledge. In the seventeenth and eighteenth centuries, several influential Scottish texts on law were produced by great thinkers: in 1655 there was Craig's feudal law book, *Jus Feudale*; then Stair's *The Institutions of the Law of Scotland* (1681), and of course David Hume's writings on criminal law.

The branches of Scots law are formed from the basic split of **public** and **private** law, as they are in England in one sense; public law deals with the nation, whereas private law deals with people and their relationships with each other and with institutions:

Public

The Scots law ancestor may have dealt with such topics as contract law, delict – law dealing with 'loss wrongfully caused', property, feudal (laws relating to old notions of landowner and vassal), udal law (up to 2004 when this was reformed), or intellectual property law.

Private

This is largely criminal law, and at the centre of the functions of this is the Crown Office Procurator Fiscal Service. This conducts investigations into crime and prosecutes, with the Lord Advocate at the top heading the Crown Office. The two occupations of procurator fiscal and advocate depute will occur frequently in research.

In terms of legal education in more recent times, passes in university courses on Scots Law were made compulsory in 1926, and in 1961 the LL.B degree was obligatory as an entry into a profession in law. As Paul Maharg of the University of Strathclyde has recently written, 'The history and culture of legal education in Scotland has developed out of an educational and university tradition almost 600 years old that was always distinctively different to that of England . . . take for instance, the four-year honours degree, a unique blend of general education and specialism.' (see 'The Scottish legal education context' at www.Ukcle.ac.uk/resources/Scotland/context.html)

We have a vivid insight into legal training and work in the late eighteenth century with the case of the great novelist, Sir Walter Scott, who was trained as an advocate in Edinburgh; his biography allows us to see the nature of the cultural context around Scots lawyers at the time. One biographer, S Fowler Wright, has this to say:

The younger advocates, idling for their opportunities around the door of the court, formed themselves into a loosely organised club, which became known as the Mountain, of which Scott was a very popular member. He still carried the nickname of his college days – Duns Scotus, in recognition of his antiquarian zeal . . .

Scott qualified, and his first case was an ecclesiastical one: a minister in Galloway had been charged with a number of scandalous affairs, and Scott, for five guineas, pleaded the man's cause. The accused was a drunkard and he had formed the habit of singing bawdy songs. Scott tried to argue that two Latin words meaning 'being drunk' and 'being drunken' should be used in the defence, and of course he failed. His biographer remarked that, 'Scott was less fitted by temperament to be a barrister than a judge. He saw both sides. He would be a poor advocate of a poor cause.' But in his biography we have an insight into the professional education of an advocate at the time.

Sources for Scotland

The main sources are at the National Archives of Scotland (NAS), but the first step is to check the standard reference works: The *Law Lists* carry Scottish details, and *The Scottish Law Directory* has been in existence since 1889. A look at the summary of offices listed in the former publication for 'Scottish law courts and offices' will show the researcher the different terminology in Scotland immediately. The Court of Session is the centre of the system, with four sittings annually and the list for 1931, for instance, shows thirteen Lords in the Inner House and the Outer House, with four deputy clerks, two for each house. As with the English entries in the Law List, the typical listing has position, name, qualification or title, (and salary in the case of the Lords):

High Court of Justiciary
Solicitor-General   John Charles Watson K.C.
Clerk of Justiciary   J R Christie O.B.E., K.C.
Depute and first assistant Alex. Rae

The *Law List* also has extensive listings of the sheriffs, sheriff-substitutes, sheriff-clerks and Fiscal Counties in Scotland. Some explanation is needed here of the courts across the counties:

MAIN LOCAL COURT: Sheriff Court JURISDICTION: Civil and Criminal.
TWO JUDGES: Judge Ordinary = Sheriff substitute / Sheriff = appeal judge.
CIVIL QUESTIONS: jurisdiction unlimited in financial terms – the money value of the cause.
CRIMINAL SIDE: Deals with all serious crime except murder.

OFFICES
   Sheriff Clerk – clerk of the Sheriff Court (the registrar in English courts) **Lord Advocate** and **Advocate Depute** prosecute in the high court, while **procurators fiscal** work in the Sheriff Court and the **convener** of the Sheriff's Court is the officer who handles petitions.

Sheriffs' records

The sheriff was the sovereign's local chief official for the law, and records of the office go back to the twelfth century. As they dealt with civil as well as criminal hearings, they were as busy as the English magistrates, but their courts began to operate alongside other courts which equate roughly to English petty sessions. By the late eighteenth century it had ceased to be a hereditary office and was salaried; the sheriff deputes came on the scene: these were qualified advocates. In the nineteenth century their duties once again broadened, to include such affairs as small debts, maritime cases and bankruptcies.

The records at the NAS are vast, embracing a wide variety of material but the most useful for family history will be court books and registers, fatal accident enquiries, registers of deed and protests and commissary records. Online, there is a tabular summary of the courts across Scotland, with record references.

Scottish Law Directory

The most comprehensive listing is for the Faculty of Advocates, and that includes these professions:

Dean of Faculty
Vice-Dean
Treasurer
Clerk of Faculty
Keeper of the Library
Clerk to Examiners and Depute Clerk of Faculty

A typical entry reads in this way, with name, qualifications, responsibilities/posts held and date of admission:

Barr, K G., M.A. LL.B. Sheriff of South Strathclyde, Dumfries and Galloway at Dumfries 1964.

But there is much more: the Sheriffdoms are listed, all the courts and clerks staff, and an extended list of country practitioners. The depth of detail may be appreciated if it is noted that each administration list for all courts finds a place here, such as:

Scottish Land Court
1, Grosvenor Crescent, Edinburgh EH12
Chairman – The Hon. Lord Elliott

Members – A. Gillespie, D. D. Mcdiarmid, A. B. Campbell
Principal Clerk – K.H.R. Graham
Depute-Clerks of Court and Senior Legal Assessors – J.G. Riddoch
and J. F. Rankin

For country practitioners, the list are numerous, and the entries give simply name, firm and address: 'Costello, J (John A Bryan and Co.) 14, Almada Street, Hamilton.

There are other sources, obvious ones in standard reference works, and some are very useful indeed if the dates of the ancestor's working life are known. The main ones are:

Kelly's Directories

Directories are invaluable for all kinds of reasons. Kelly's, for Glasgow in 1961, for instance, has listings of officers in the Scottish courts, including staff working at Airdrie and Hamilton. The entry gives the days of the week on which courts were held at that time (even the Small Debt Court) and then lists legal professionals, such as:

Sheriff of Lanarkshire: A G Walker Q.C.

Substitutes: W J Bryden, H W Pirie, F Middleton, N D MacLeod, J Bayne, T A U Wood, S E Bell, C H Johnston, QC, J M Peterson, W O Patullo, J I Smith, J A Forsyth, Q.C. & P G B McNeill

The *Scots Law Times*

This is an invaluable publication, giving obituaries, but perhaps more important, it has business changes sections, so that, again, if dates are known of the ancestor's period of work, movements may be traced. A typical entry for 'Business Changes' reads (1961 edition):

Messrs MacRobert Son and Hutchison, Solicitors, Paisley and Glasgow intimate that they have assumed Mr John Henderson Greene, M.A. LL.B., as partner in their firm.

The obituaries are normally brief and exact:

Mr L. J. Craigie, W.S., Edinburgh
On 21st March 1961, Laurence John Craigie. W.S. Edinburgh
[W. S. = Writer to the Signet [see the following case study]]

The *Scots Law Times* is a publication that offers all kinds of insights into the practice of law in Scotland, a real professional journal, with various dimensions of practice and training incorporated.

Biographical Dictionaries

In the nineteenth century, there were large numbers of popular biographical dictionaries and these will often have lawyers included in fairly major proportions. Of course they are usually the more elevated members of the profession. Typical is *A Biographical Dictionary of Eminent Scotsmen*, published by Nimmo's of Edinburgh. Here is an entry:

ABERCROMBIE
    The honourable Alexander, Lord Abercrombie, a distinguished lawyer in the latter part of the eighteenth century, and an elegant occasional writer . . . In May 1792 he was appointed one of the judges of the Court of Session . . .

There is also the *Dictionary of Scottish Biography* by Kenneth Roy (Carrick, 1999).

The Stair Society

The Stair Society (taking its name from the great legal theorist, James Dalrymple, Viscount Stair) was formed in 1934 'to encourage the study and to advance the knowledge of the history of Scots law'. As an equivalent of the English Selden Society, it publishes volumes on legal history, defined by the Society as 'a significant body of historical material, most of which is not otherwise readily available to lawyers or historians'. Some of these publications are academic and theoretical but there are a number of volumes which provide biographical information about lawyers. An undoubtedly valuable

William Dalrymple, Lord Stair, from Lives of Eminent Scotsmen, *1890.*
Author's collection

volume in this respect is *The Minute Book of the Faculty of Advocates* – a series covering much of the eighteenth century, edited by Angus Stewart. The most recent book in the series, covering the years 1783–1978 is edited by Stewart and Dr David Parratt (2007).

Other relevant and useful volumes are:

The Court book of the Barony and Regality of Falkirk and Callendar Vol. 1 1638–1656. This is edited by Doreen M Hunter (1991).

The Records of the Synod of Lothian and Tweeddale Vol. 1 1661–1712, edited by James Kirk, 1977.

The Justiciary Records of Argyll and the Isles 1664–1742, edited by John Imrie, (1969).

Selected Justiciary Cases 1624–1650, edited by Stair A Gillon (1953).

The National Archives of Scotland (NAS)

These archives hold various categories of records of interest to family historians. The main ones are Justice of the Peace records, comprising minute books, records of quarter sessions, records of licensing courts, courts books from petty sessions, clerks' letter books, appeals and testimonials. These are all in a series beginning JP1 and going to JP37, covering all regions of Scotland, although a few are in the City Archives of Glasgow, Aberdeen or Stirling.

Persistence is required for a search, but if the search terms 'lawyers' records' and 'solicitors' records' are used, then details of major records such as the Exchequer Courts are listed, (in the series E851–E867) and also there are listings of firms of solicitors with dates, such as 'Glen and Henderson, Lothian, 1823–1929' or at GD237, 'Papers of Messrs Tods, Murray and Jamieson, lawyers of Edinburgh' – with an incredible date range of 1331–1937. As with the English A2A, a search for law firms at the NAS can be very productive.

There are also General Minute Books at CS16 & 17 covering 1661 to 1835 in manuscript. Minute books for 1782–1990 are at CS17/1. These are excellent as a starting point for a lawyer, because the lawyer's name is on each entry. Once an action was begun, the same clerk was at work at each stage of the process. The Court of Session card index at the Archives will be consulted via the Clerk of Session's abbreviation for the case record.

Helpfully, there is a research guide for each main criminal record type online at the NAS. But there is a large volume of material in print as well and these are listed online. For instance, the registers of the Privy Council, and of the Great Seal, the Acts of the Lords in Council on Civil Cases, are all there in print. There is the massive resource for earlier centuries of the Exchequer Rolls of Scotland covering the years 1264–1600. This is in 22 volumes, edited by John Stuart and George Burnett.

To trace any lawyers in cases at the Court of Session before 1660, check the General Minute Books at CS8, and for cases after that date, consult CS12/13/14. The research guides online give full directions for references. These are clear and well presented, with terms explained (www.nas.gov.uk/guides/introductionToProcesses.asp).

It should also be mentioned, with the vocabulary of law in mind, that the NAS site also has a glossary of legal terms. Included in the bibliography section in the present work is a law glossary, incorporating the principal terms from Scottish legal professions, but once again, it must be stressed that for this particular family history subject, a dictionary of law is needed on your desk as you work.

The Irish State and its law

As early as 1210, when King John was in Ireland, there was an order that the Common Law be imprinted there, and the existing native system of law, called the *brehon*, was dropped. There was, in these earlier centuries, the use of royal writs and an assize system; but by 1612 the English Common Law was general in Ireland. There was a royal representative, as in England, termed the justiciar. But it was not until 1877 that the courts system described below was established.

Up to 1921, the body of statutes created in England had force in Ireland, then with the establishment of the Irish Free State, a fresh system was introduced, so although there were legal structures in Ireland, as in Scotland, influenced by the Norman invasions in the early Middle Ages, the organisation of courts and professionals since

1877 has an identity all its own. At the centre, the judges are appointed by the President and Council of Advisers.

In 1922, the constitution of the Irish Free State had an inclusion regarding a judiciary being formed, and previously there had been Dail Courts – various courts with full scope of all levels of legal business from parish to the Supreme Court. These were now superseded.

The Courts (Establishment and Constitution) Act of 1961 formally instituted the system summarised here, done in accordance with Article 34 of the 1937 Constitution.

At the everyday level there is the District Court and there are twenty-three districts, with forty-six judges overall. A District Court judge, sitting as in an English magistrates' court with only the judge and not a jury, deals with lesser criminal offences. At a higher level there is the Circuit Court, and there are eight circuits, so the method of work is similar to the old assizes in England; there is one President of the Court and a group of seventeen judges with him, and the functions may be civil, criminal and appeal, and again, as with assizes, there is a twelve-person jury.

The superior court, the High Court, has determining powers in civil and criminal law, and the official name is the Central Criminal Court. In Dublin today, studying the locations of various courts which have been in existence there over the centuries can be confusing; as with gaols, there have been so many and with such different functions, so in tracing ancestors, some historical knowledge will help, and reading court reports from past times will be useful in this exercise. There is also the institution of the Special Criminal Court (the major court in Dublin, in Green Street), that has special use today when required, the purpose being to ensure that there is justice done without interference: something that is notably a product of the unstable history of Ireland in terms of factions and civil war of course. Three judges sit at that court, and there is no jury: there is one judge from each of the other courts – District, Circuit and High, at that assembly. As in England, there is a Court of Criminal Appeal, again with three judges, but all from superior courts.

Above all this, there is the Supreme Court for final appeal, and there the judgements are made with the decision of studying the nature of the constitution of the state on the one hand and the sentences from statutes made in previous courts.

As to the legal profession: there are solicitors and barristers as in England, and solicitors handle matters such as commercial law, land law and probate, working in court mostly in District contexts. Barristers work in higher courts, and they are either junior or senior counsel.

The two chief professional bodies are The Incorporated Law Society of Ireland, founded in 1852, which regulates the solicitor's profession, and the Benchers of the Honorable Society of King's Inns operate in the same way for the Irish Bar. In some contemporary accounts, there are descriptions of what the barristers and judges in Ireland were like at particular times. For instance, Michael McCarthy wrote an account of Ireland in the years 1895–1900 and he states that in that period there were 1,077 men in Ireland called to the Bar. His explanation of the profession gives the researcher an excellent insight into their work:

Strangers say that the method of transacting business adopted by the Irish barristers is unique. Instead of each man having an office and a clerk in the vicinity of the courts, or in a central position in town, they all sit or stand in one room from 10 to 5 daily during term, except when engaged in court. The bag of briefs and papers is sent down early from the barrister's house on the shoulders of some seedy . . . male loafer and the bag may be seen finding its devious way home similarly at night.

As to solicitors at the same time, McCarthy notes that there were then, again, around 1,500, and that 'The whole scheme of legal administration . . . was originally well thought out, but I fear is getting out of touch with the people.' He comments that the Bill of Costs related to solicitors' work then was a challenge to understand: 'The most abstruse thesis in dogmatic theology does not stun the brain as does one of those bills.'

Sources for Ireland

The fact that Ireland had very much the English system for so long is fortunate for the family historian. This has meant that law reports in the national and regional press across the United Kingdom always covered courts in Dublin and other areas of Ireland along with the English and Welsh reports. Even towns such as Nenagh in County Tipperary had their trials reported, and English readers throughout the centuries were well informed on penal matters, criminal activities and police work in Ireland as much as they were informed about the lives and affairs of lawyers in the courts. The reasons are not hard to find: they relate of course to the troubled political history of Ireland, from pro-French insurrection to Fenianism and Sinn Fein.

Law Reports/Digest of cases

A glance at the Law Reports for Ireland will show the lists of the judges in the courts. For instance, in 1969 under the Act referred to above (for 1961), the judges in the Supreme Court between 1961 and 1969 were just eight, and in the same period, the various reports list judges in Supreme Court, High Court and the Attorney General. The Law Reports cover the Incorporated Council of Law Reporting for Ireland, The Incorporated Council of Law Reporting for Northern Ireland, *The Irish Law Times* and *The Irish Jurist*. For the last two sources, as with the Scottish equivalents, names of barristers and solicitors are given with reports, obituaries and employment references with particular firms.

Parliamentary Papers

There is much that will be valuable for family historians in the British Parliamentary Papers. A search in the general indexes of bills, reports, estimates and enquiries will prove useful. The categories of material which would be most useful are reports of royal commissions, official correspondence on crime and law, and commissions of enquiry. All these will have the names of solicitors and barristers, as well as of judges, for the period of the historian's trawl of information on a particular legal professional. Basically there were always statements made by a large number of qualified people in the profession which were used in the papers. The most helpful guide to these, with the Irish context in mind, is in Brian Griffin's handbook: *Sources for the Study of Crime in Ireland 1801–1921* (Four Courts Press, Dublin, 2006).

The National Archives of Ireland (NAI)

The records are somewhat scattered, but searches under the sub-heading of the Crown and Peace section brings a useful summary of records held. The office of the Crown and Peace had two separate offices: the office of Clerk of the Crown and the office of Clerk of the Peace. These are rather akin to the justices in England, and they were appointed by the *custos rotulorum*, the keeper of rolls and records for a county.

The people in these records were therefore Clerks of assizes, and the records will register the people who acted in the courts as solicitors, and the Clerk also had coroners' returns, so the coroners will be named and referred to from this same database.

With regard to barristers, the records are hard to find, but there are some key sections, such as for the period 1946–69 which is covered by Reference 8/456/3 – and has qualifications of barristers and solicitors, judges and court officers. The opinions of candidates by the Attorney General is included.

Lawyers' Yeomanry Corps

In the Regency period, with the threat of French invasion and in-surrection by various ranks of nationalists, the yeomanry regiments were formed in Ireland. The records are scattered, but the chances are that if your ancestor was a lawyer in Ireland in the years c.1790–1820, he will have been in the lawyers' yeomanry or some other corps. The Lawyers' Yeomanry Corps are known to have been active, for instance, against the patriot Robert Emmet (himself a lawyer). At the Public Record Office of Northern Ireland in the Local

Studies there are papers relating to lawyers in these forces, as in Local History Series 1796 LA 25/244/3 and 4. At TNA, Kew, there are various sources, including PRO Class HO60, boxes 1–19, relating to the years 1820–40. More specifically, PRO 30/9/115 has papers of Dr Charles Lindsay who was linked to the Dublin yeomanry in 1801, and these are supplemented by records at Dublin Castle.

For an account of the Dublin lawyers' corps, see the article by Kenneth Ferguson, 'The Irish Bar in December, 1798' in *Dublin Historical Record* Vol. 52 No.1 (Spring, 1999), pp. 32–60.

Biographical reference

In print, there is a work by Joseph Constantine Smyth which covers details and dates of all important legal professionals in Ireland before 1814, and the people included were working in Northern Ireland as well as England. This is *The Chronicle of the Law Officers of Ireland*. The description in the contents summary explains in full:

Containing lists of the lord chancellors and keepers of the Great Seal, masters of the rolls, chief justices and judges of the courts of King's Bench, Common Pleas and Exchequer, attorneys and solicitors general with the serjeants-at-law, from the earliest period; dates and abstracts of their patents; fees and allowances from the Crown, tenures of office, with the promotions, deaths or resignations from the reign of Queen Elizabeth to the present time. Judges' salaries in 1690 . . .

There are also newspaper archives, and a rich source of information is in the indexes to biographical writing in newspapers. These are some of the main sources in this context:

National Library of Ireland indexes to: *Freeman's Journal* (1763–1771) and the index to marriages and deaths in *Pue's Occurrences* and in *The Dublin Gazette* (for the years 1730–1740). The *Hibernian Magazine* 1772–1812, with biographical notices, and card indexes to the *Hibernian Chronicle* for 1771–1800 and *The Cork Mercantile Chronicle* (1803–1818). Both are available at The Irish Genealogical Society.

For Northern Ireland, there are:

The *Belfast Newsletter* (1737–1800) in the Linenhall Library (see bibliography) and the list of article references produced by the Southern Education and Library Board. These have an index with personal names included.

Special mention must be made of some writings by Rosemary Folliott: *The Index to Biographical Notices Collected from Newspapers* (mainly for Cork and Kerry); these are for the years 1756–1827, and *The Index to Biographical Notices in the Newspapers of Limerick, Ennis, Clonmel and Waterford*, for 1758–1821.

More details of these biographical sources may be found at the website of the *Irish Times*: www.irishtimes.com/ancestor/browse/records/news/indexes.htm

The Public Record Office of Northern Ireland (PRONI)

This organisation has all kinds of archives of use to family historians, and there is a very useful online index of privately deposited archives. This is an excellent source if you know the family name and/or the approximate dates and county in which the ancestor worked. For instance, the alphabetical list of private papers brings up the Porter family papers, which include the Falls and Hanna archive: a solicitor's firm with materials covering the years 1830–1950. They were a family from Enniskillen and the material is substantial. Similarly, the Andrews Papers, from Ardara, County Down, include papers from the man who was a judge of the Exchequer in 1882. At the very top of the professional tree, there are also the Cherry Papers: Richard Cherry was Attorney-General of Ireland during 1905–1909. All guides and introductions at the PRONI site are very clear and it is a quick task to home in on the period or name you want.

On a wider scale, there are helpful lists of papers and topics on all aspects of legal records such as probate and wills. In a Local History Series, there is a list of subjects with specific guides, such as for Armagh the Armagh Diocesan Archive, which includes law topics and records of the prerogative courts.

Directories

As usual in family history, the local directories provide perhaps the very best first steps in obtaining the basic facts of an ancestor's profession. There were several varieties of directory for Dublin and for other major cities or towns in Ireland, and recently Dublin Public Library Publications has produced a facsimile of a very early example: *A Directory of Dublin for the Year 1738* (2006).

Other useful ones are *Pettigrew and Oulton's Dublin Almanac*, and some of these are searchable online. The 1842 edition has simple listings of names but also categories under the headings Barristers-at-Law, Commissioners and Attorneys. Therefore there will be plain entries under the main directory of names such as:

Worthington, Richard, solicitor, 10, Charles St. Gt.

But then under the main legal headings we have, under Barristers-at-Law, these kinds of entries:

	Admitted
Acheson, J Gilman, 40 Hardwicke Street	E 1837
Adair, John H Mountjoy, Sq. south	T 1835
Adams, John, 56, Eccles Street	M 1828

(E, T and M refer respectively to the law terms of Easter, Trinity and Michaelmas, the other term being Hilary)

There is also *Shaw's Dublin City Directory*, with similar entries, so that solicitors are included thus: 'Sparks, F H 196, Great Brunswick Street, solicitor.' But the publication also has a separate *Law Directory*.

Case Study: Writer to the Signet

This profession is the oldest body of law practitioners in Scotland, working in the Scottish Supreme Courts in a way rather similar to that of solicitors in England. One of the most famous Writers of the Signet is probably the crime writer, William Roughead (1870–1952). He edited several learned volumes in the series published by Hodge of Edinburgh and Glasgow, under the title *Notable Scottish Trials*, and he sat in virtually all the high-profile murder trials in Scotland

William Roughead, author and Writer to the Signet. Author's collection

between 1900 and 1950. Roughead, born in Edinburgh, began his legal studies in 1889 and joined the class studying Civil Law. He passed the examinations in that subject in 1890, and then entered the class for Scots Law the next year. By the session of 1891–182 he was in the class for Conveyancing, and he worked with a firm to attain his articled status: a company called TS MacLaren, William Traquair,

Junior, at 11, Hill Street in Edinburgh. He did the second year in the Conveyancing class, and as his biographer, Richard Whittington-Egan, wrote: 'He sat his Conveyancing examination in 1893, came thirty-fifth in his class, and earned a second meritorious mention in the University Calendar.'

In July 1893, he was admitted as a member of the Society of Writers to Her Majesty's Signet. He had an office at 122 George Street, then later moved to number 13, and there he was entrenched until 1947.

In his duties as a Writer to the Signet he was one of a special society of law agents, originally clerks in the office of the Secretary of State, and even today, all summons papers are signed on the last page by a Writer to the Signet. The Signet was originally the private seal of the first Kings of Scotland, and the Writers were the official body of clerks who were authorised to supervise and then sign court documents. The earliest recorded instance of the Signet being used was in 1369. When the College of Justice was formed in 1532, Writers to the Signet were part of that establishment. The College of Justice is the group of courts under and part of the Supreme Courts of Scotland; the Court is led by the Lord President, and the professional bodies of lawyers are all associated: the Faculty of Advocates, the Society of Writers to the Signet and the Society of Solicitors. The College was created by the Parliament of Scotland Act which authorised the college, with fourteen original members.

But it was not until 1594 that the Keeper of the Signet, the highest court secretary, gave commissions to other men – those who would be the first recognisably modern Writers.

There is no charter, but after the 1707 Union, the point for discussion was whether or not the Writers would be admitted to the Scottish bench, but although it was allowed after a period of ten years at work, there has only been one recorded Writer who has taken such a seat – a certain Hamilton of Pencaitland in 1712.

The essential nature of the position is that the Writer, with a broad knowledge of Scots law, also has to be well informed in aspects of law, from jurisprudence to the more administrative and scholarly elements of legal work. All this knowledge is what lies behind the notion of a person signing a document in an official capacity. It is

GLASGOW

ABERDEEN

EDINBURGH

DUNDEE

THE JURIDICAL REVIEW

The Law Journal of Scottish Universities

1980 PART 1—JUNE

Frustration of Contract

Effect of a Pardon in Scots Law

" Despotism of Law " in an Agricultural Community

Legal Obligation and the Moral Nature of Law

Defamation by a Judge ? Fixing the Limits

Case & Comment

The Juridical Review, *prestigious Scots law journal. Author's collection* perhaps best explained by referring to the famous story of the painter James Whistler who, when in court and asked by the counsel who was prosecuting John Ruskin why he was asking two hundred guineas for two days' labour, replied, 'No, I ask it for the knowledge of a lifetime.'

Arguably, William Roughead is an exceptional, rather than a typical example of a Writer to the Signet, but the important point is that he had studied law: he was not an amateur. This is ably demonstrated in his many contributions to the highly-regarded journal, *The Juridical Review*. Luc Sante, who edited a selection of Roughead's writing, wrote: 'He began his career at twenty-three as a Writer to the Signet, a term that has no literary implication, referring rather to an elite body of Scottish attorneys. His passion for the law extended well beyond his actual duties . . . '

The researcher looking into Scottish lawyer ancestors will find that comment a helpful insight: the cultural and literary interests are never far away in the lives of Scots lawyers in Edinburgh. There has to have been an influence from that on how they viewed the legal process in action, in the human community.

Chapter Ten
APPROACHES AND METHODS:
A SUMMARY

As has surely become evident, tracing an ancestor in any of the legal professions is a considerable challenge. The features of the sources and resources for this are that they are disparate, often accessible only by indirect means, and certainly in the case of country solicitors, hidden away in local archives. For barristers in England (and consequently for judges and higher offices) there is less difficulty. But for the various legal occupations such as clerks and former offices such as proctors or sheriffs, the sources are there but they are often obscure.

However, what has been demonstrated so far is that, with perseverance, they may be found. The process is generally this:

Phase 1

Start with the span of dates and look at newspapers (local and national) and also directories and almanacs. Name searches in secondary sources may follow. The availability of indexes will vary from place to place.

Phase 2

Go to local or regional sources, or specialist ones for the particular profession involved. The Victorian almanacs will always provide a first step, and monographs by local history societies will help also.

Phase 3

Then look at the other options. For instance, if the person was active only in London, then there will be a number of potential sources in the major archives, most promisingly at the London Metropolitan Archives and of course in the Law Society material.

Naturally, the rationale is based on the context in time: for ancestors before the Early Modern period, the sources will be more difficult to find because either they are in obscure places or they were not primarily involved in anything noteworthy. There may be only names on documents or in lists of court offices in many cases.

Later, with both newspapers and secondary sources in directories to go on, there is more chance that the ancestor was a little more prominent and 'visible' in records. The online resources continue to grow and more openings occur every day. Of course the legal profession, as has been demonstrated above, includes many sub-groups, and from the mid-nineteenth century the references in source books are either by occupation (in basic listings) or by name, even if there is simply a minimal entry in an obituary.

Summary of procedures for the main categories:

Barristers and Judges

For these professions, the sources are in all professional and general reference works with official listings; also there will be numerous mentions in newspaper archives and in records of major societies. The large volume of memoir literature will also be worth looking at.

Solicitors and Attorneys/Notaries

The most fruitful source will be County Record Office archives and A2A would therefore be the first step to locate the sources you need by category. In addition to that, there are The National Archive resources and research guides. The most direct first approach is to consult Amanda Bevan's book, *Tracing Your Ancestors in The National Archives* (see bibliography).

For barristers, solicitors, attorneys, notaries and proctors, the perspective will be Medieval and Early Modern, as well as taking in the age of the periodical and the newspaper from the early eighteenth century, so therefore the sources will be diverse in the publications of record societies, scholarly legal history publications, and again, The National Archives.

Other legal professions

Here, the multiplicity of materials is the challenge, and so the most sensible first step is to use the directories and almanacs, and then add to that court reports, obituaries and local history sources. In many cases (as in scriveners) there are professional associations and specialist libraries to consult also.

Quick help alternatives

The Black Sheep Index

An additional resource, always worth checking, is the online Black Sheep Index. This provides lists of names, by category, including lawyers, and the material listed refers to newspaper reports in the period; the main 'Black and White Sheep' list is defined as 'people involved with the law' and legal professionals are included. For instance, under Clark we have **Clark, David, Dundee, Solicitor, 1906.** That means that there is a newspaper entry or feature on him at that date. For a small fee the article may be ordered (£8 at the time of writing, 2009/10).

This is undoubtedly a very handy resource, also including lists of criminals and police officers. As long as the researcher knows the full name of the ancestor, there is a fair chance that something useful will emerge.

Obscure Autobiographies

If the ancestor has been involved in any kind of public event, the basic reports in the newspaper archives will send the search into other, lateral sources, and the out-of-print memoirs of lawyers and related officials may prove worthwhile for consultation. The immediate sources for these are the specialist crime and criminology booksellers. The two most prominent in England are Clifford Elmer Books and Loretta Lay Books (London). Both have searchable online catalogues.

Family History/Local History Societies

The Federation of Family History Societies is always worth a look and the chat rooms and query pages are fertile ground. The website for the FFHS has a section for archives liaison, a discussion forum and an ezine.

The British Association for Local History (BALH) has some very helpful materials. There is an index and collection of abstracts to publications and all articles in the journal, and this is *Unlocking the Past* by Alan Crosby (2001). Local history specialists often have very narrowly defined interest and their passion for knowledge has often extended over many years. Trades and professions frequently figure in these enquiries.

A2A Search

The massive Access to Archives resource is always worth a determined search, using a range of key words. Experience shows that a general term such as 'firms of solicitors' or 'scriveners' will bring a considerable list, and although time is required to trawl through, the pleasure of knowledge attained by serendipity will always be a possibility.

British History Online

This is an immense resource and the resources for legal ancestors are massive and diverse. Search terms are the key to success: a broad category such as 'notaries' will bring all kinds of material, and a restricted search by dates will of course help. There is also the county reference listings, so that regional enquiries may be made. Overall,

Law Notes

A

MONTHLY MAGAZINE

FOR

PRACTITIONERS AND STUDENTS

VOL. LXVII.

LONDON:

"LAW NOTES" PUBLISHING OFFICES, 25 & 26, CHANCERY LANE.

1948

Frontispiece for Law Notes, *1948. Author's collection*

with its huge parliamentary records database, this is excellent for all categories of records for legal professionals.

The Annual Register

This digest of information on politics, economics, law and military affairs always had, since its inception in the mid-eighteenth century, an emphasis on factual information on several aspects of crime and justice. Issues have trial reports, summaries of the law terms, sessions and assize reports, and obituaries. Later volumes are indexed also. Some volumes have special features on legal topics (as does *The British Almanac*).

GLOSSARY

Note: For further clarification of legal terms, the family historian is advised to consult one of the student law dictionaries or general dictionaries available. There are several to choose from, but my references throughout this book have been either to *Osborn's Concise Law Dictionary*, edited by Mick Woodley, or to *Mozley and Whiteley's Law Dictionary*, ninth edition, edited by John B Saunders. (Both are listed below.) Law tends to be one of those subjects in which a search for explanations of terms often leads to the appearance of other terms (many of them abstract concepts) and a lateral search for meaning will distract the reader. The following minimal list is consequently intended to help. If the reader absorbs these terms first, before the research, it will make the process more manageable.

The researcher will come across many of these terms in such sources as assize rolls and documents before 1500, as well as in modern text which explains the law at particular points in time. However, it is helpful to know that in the editions of legal documents and biographical materials produced by the scholarly societies mentioned in the book – such as the county record societies and the Chetham and Surtees societies – there are usually glossaries for each text.

The following list provides merely the most frequently encountered terms in research in this area. As with all family history, of course, there will be a need, with earlier sources, to have some supporting material from guides to handwriting and spelling etc.

Advocate   A person who pleads for another in a court of law. There was a College of Advocates until 1857.

Advocates, Faculty of   The body which appoints advocates in Scotland, also appointing members of the Bar.

Amercement   Convicted offenders were in the King's mercy and were liable to pay a cash penalty – an amercement.

Assizes   The courts held in the towns in the county circuits, where judges would travel from Westminster to hear cases.

Attainder   In the medieval period, offenders sentenced to death or banishment were subject to attaint: they lost their land and even their heirs were under the same attainder.

Attorney   A term equivalent to that of solicitor, notably linked to the Courts of King's Bench and Common Pleas. From 1729, attorneys could also be admitted to practise in Chancery.

Barrister   A lawyer who works in the courts, the name deriving from the original 'bar' of the court, beyond which the law students sat, to watch and learn.

Bencher   The alternative name is Master of the Bench, and this refers to the governing body of the various Inns of Court.

Central Criminal Court   ('The Old Bailey') The court in London which heard cases from London, Middlesex and some areas of Essex. But it integrated with the High Court in 1875.

Chancery, Court of   A court hearing petitions to the sovereign in council. It also had jurisdiction in common law.

Clerk of the Peace   The administrator for the Justice of the Peace at quarter sessions.

Commission of Oyez and Terminer   A commission to 'hear and determine' cases at court on indictment, and these handled serious crime, notably at assizes.

Common Law   The old, unwritten law of England. This has always been expressed in legal decisions, in distinction from law made by statute.

Common Pleas   The court which was originally part of the King's Court – the *Curia Regis*.

Common Serjeant   A judicial officer of the City of London.

Consistory Court   The Bishop's ecclesiastical court.

Coroner   An office which has been in existence since 1194, then the 'crowner' – the central responsibility being to supervise at inquests.

Court Leet   The court of a manor dealing with offences of a petty nature. Some leet records have been printed (see the Chetham Society).

Crown Court   This was created by the Courts Act of 1971, displacing the assizes and quarter sessions.

Deposition   A statement used to give written or spoken evidence, not read at a trial except in cases where the witness cannot be produced in court by the counsel.

Disseisin   A dispossession (usually of land).

Doctors' Commons   A residence for civil law lawyers, also having the Court of Arches, the Admiralty High Court and the Bishop of London's Consistory Court.

Ecclesiastical Courts   Courts regulated and formed by the church. These could be in the form of the Archdeacon's court, the Bishop's (consistory) court or the commissary court.

Examiner   An official – a barrister – appointed to examine witnesses, so ordered by the Lord Chancellor

Exchequer, Court   This was the court, dating from early medieval times, handling the King's accounts, and the officers who handled debts owed to the King were called the King's Remembrancer and the Treasurer's Remembrancer.

Felony   The category of crime which was in common law serious enough for the transgressor to forfeit land and chattels. In 1870 the Forfeiture Act ended this. In plain terms, it meant an offence for which a jury trial was necessary.

Great Seal   The Lord Chancellor's seal, which is applied to verify writs at elections, or in foreign treaties.

Honorial Courts   An honor was the collection of estates owned by a tenant-in-chief of the King, and the Normans permitted such people to have their own special courts.

Inns of Court   The places in which barristers were trained and housed, a university of a kind; the Inns are: Gray's Inn, Lincoln's Inn, the Middle Temple and the Inner Temple, all in London.

Judicature, Supreme Court   This was formed after the Act of 1873 which brought together the high courts of justice and appeal.

Jurors   A property qualification for jurors was first established in 1285. Then in 1692 a statute enacted that the juror had to have a freehold or life tenure to the value of at least £10 a year. From 1730 leaseholders having property worth £20 per annum were included in the jury lists. Lists of jurors were given to quarter sessions. Then, from 1825, jury service was restricted to people between 21 and 60 who had freehold property with a value of £20 a year or who had property worth £30 per annum.

Justice of the Peace   (also magistrate) Local justices, first appointed, as 'keepers' of the peace in 1327. The term Justice of the Peace was created in 1361.

Justiciar   The origins of this very high office lie in the early twelfth century; the King, away from home, needed a representative, and so the justiciar was established, the first being Roger, Bishop of Salisbury, in 1120.

Legal executive   The non-admitted staff of a solicitor.

Lord Lieutenant   This is the office which is defined as being the ruler's chief representative in each county of England.

Marshal   An officer who, formerly, assisted the judge at assizes. He swore in the grand jury in criminal cases, and in civil cases, he took records and monitored causes.

Misdemeanour   An offence not relating to a felony. Punishment was by a fine or imprisonment. The Criminal Law Act of 1967 abolished the distinction between a felony and a misdemeanour.

Muniments   Title deeds relating to land.

Nisi Prius   (literally meaning 'unless before') This is a judicial writ which gave the sheriff of a shire the power to gather a jury for a civil action to the court at Westminster on a given day 'unless before' the time that justices came to the assize town. If that happened, the jury would be assembled at the assize. Barristers and judges would sit at these courts, and they were usually dealing with serious and pressing matters, so press reports were substantial.

Notary Public   A legal official who attests deeds and other documents, and who also makes copies of the documents.

Oath Rolls   People having a public office, between Tudor times and the mid-Victorian years, had to swear allegiance on an oath roll, to the Crown, and also to the Church of England.

Prerogative Court   The Court of Canterbury, the court of probate for the Archbishop of Canterbury.

Presentment   The report of a jury relating to an offence brought to its attention; or a report to a manorial court.

Proctor   The solicitor acting within the ecclesiastical courts.

Procurator Fiscal   In Scotland, the officer of the sheriff's court who looks into offences within the area of jurisdiction; he is a prosecutor also.

Quarter Sessions   The meetings of the county justices held four times each year.

Recorder   A barrister appointed to work with justices.

Registrar   An officer who registers the decrees of a court of justice, or who keeps registers of actions and events.

Remembrancer   An Officer of the Exchequer. There were three up until 1925: the Queen's, the Lord Treasurer's and the Remembrancer of First Fruits. When the researcher consults TNA for material on rolls for instance, the word 'remembrancer' will be found there. The Queen's Remembrancer logs all materials relating to debts to the Crown and to issue processes for the Customs. The Treasurer's and First Fruits remembrancers have the primary duty of reporting to the Lord Treasurer anything of important matters relating to the sovereign.

Replevin   A writ of restitution.

Serjeants-at-Law   Barristers who are admitted to the Order of the Coif. They are commanded to that status by order of the Great Seal.

Sheriff   Originally the 'shire reeve' and this office was, before the creation of the Lord Lieutenant, the sovereign's main representative in the counties.

Solicitor   Originally, these were officers of the Court of Chancery, but after 1873, all attorneys, solicitors and proctors were termed solicitors of the Supreme Court.

Star Chamber   A court re-established in 1487 by Henry VII, after it had fallen into disuse (it is a very old institution). Privy Councillors, lords spiritual and temporal, sat with two common law judges and no jury, to try serious crime throughout the Tudor dynasty and into the early Stuart years, being abolished in 1640.

Steward   A Crown officer who formerly supervised a manorial or other court.

Terms   The terms used for the legal sittings of the year at assizes: Hilary, Easter, Trinity and Michaelmas.

Vestry Clerk   The official who kept minutes and dealt with the organisation of the vestry business.

Writ   The official, Crown-sanctioned command for something to be done and an action taken. They were either original or judicial. Original writs were sent to a defendant, and judicial writs were sent by courts and the document had the name of the justice concerned, rather than the name of the sovereign, which would be on the original writ.

Writer to the Signet (Scotland)   The oldest body of legal professionals in Scotland: they are solicitors to the Supreme Court.

BIBLIOGRAPHY AND SOURCES

Note: Included here are details of various sources for legal history, selected for these main reasons: explanations of professions and their job descriptions; help for researchers with understanding the legal context within the period of the ancestor's life and work, and for support in accessing unusual records. In addition, there are here all the important family history sources for these professions.

The lists of websites have been kept as one major list, rather than by category, but it is a simple matter to find the Irish and Scottish references from that comprehensive list. As to the related professional bodies and academic organisations, I have only listed the ones either directly relevant to the subject, or some choice secondary ones which clearly have links to law and legal history.

In every case, it is clear that the professional bodies, such as the law societies of England, Scotland and Ireland, have their own partial records, and that comprehensive references for more recent times even in the lives of barristers, are hard to assemble. Paradoxically, for barristers at the Inns of Court, records before c.1830 are more easily available in print than other legal professions or than some later records.

I have also listed some of the more anecdotal and contextual memoirs, but the ones listed all have indexes. Otherwise they would be of very little use to family historians. Many Victorian memoirs contain a great deal of useful information on the everyday lives of lawyers, and although they may be difficult to obtain, an increasing number are available online. There is also the usefulness of journal articles to consider. Articles by scholars and monographs by local historians, with small print runs, are often extremely informative on the lives of lawyers and on firms or on the history of professions in particular. I have only included a small selection of these, and readers are referred to the publications of local history societies, but also to specialist historical journals which tend to carry articles on crime and law quite frequently. These are: *Past and Present, The British Review, Social History* and *The Journal of Legal History*. In addition, *The Journal of Regional and Local History* will have useful secondary topics covered.

How to use this Resource Section

Your ancestor's life and work provide the focus of research here, so some guidance is needed on using this resources section to the best advantage. My recommendation is that these steps are taken through this compilation of sources:
1. List the main reference sources for the occupation in question.
2. Take out the information relating to dates within the life-span of your ancestor.
3. Put together the material from the wider context and then read up on the elements of the person's professional life and culture. For instance, a barrister's life and actions or involvements in work in the mid-Victorian period would entail:
   Brief biographical notes in the Inns of Court, Law Society records, oath rolls, press reports and so on; these need to be placed in context with the larger, national events such as the changes in the Bar and in the Law Society in the 1890s.
With luck, he will be mentioned in the press at certain times.

Books

Almanacs and General Reference

Annual Register (Baldwin, Craddock and Joy, 1821)
Archbold's *The Justice of the Peace and Parish officer, with the practice of Country Attorneys in Criminal Cases* (Shaw and Sons, 1854)
Biographical Dictionary of Eminent Scotsmen (Blackie and Son, Edinburgh, 1894)

The British Almanac for the year 1837 (The Society for the Diffusion of Useful Knowledge, 1837)

Calendar of Fine Rolls, preserved in the Public Record Office, 1383–1391 (HMSO, 1929)

Costin, WC and Watson, J Steven, *The Law and Working of the Constitution: Documents 1660–1914* (two volumes) (Adam and Charles Black, 1952)

Courts of Criminal Appeal (Sweet and Maxwell, 1907–1964)

Cox's Crown Cases Reserved

A Directory of Dublin for the Year 1738 (Dublin Public Libraries, 2006)

Empire Law List (annual)

Gray, John, *Lawyers' Latin: a vade mecum* (Robert Hale, 2006)

Griffin, Brian, *Primary Sources for the Study of Crime in Ireland 1821–1921* (Four Courts Press, 2005)

Irish Law Times

Kelly's Directory of Glasgow (1968 edition, referred to in text)

Law List (annual) (Stevens and Sons)

Parliamentary papers: Vol.9 *First Report of Her Majesty's Commissioners, for enquiry into the process, practice and system of Pleading in the Superior Courts of Common Law* (Eyre and Spottiswoode, 1851)

Parliamentary papers: *First Report into the Courts of Law in Scotland* (Murray and Gibb, 1869)

Parliamentary papers Vol.6 (1840) *An Act for Facilitating the Administration of Justice* (Irish University Press, 1971)

Parliamentary Papers: *Royal Commission and Select Committee on Legal Administration 1833–1845* (Shannon, Ireland, 1971)

Pettigrew and Oulton's Dublin Almanac (1842)

Ryan, Edward F, *The Law Reports of the Incorporated Council of Law Reporting for Ireland: Digest of Cases*

The Scots Law Times (W Green and Sons, Edinburgh)

Scottish Law Directory (annual) (William Hodge, Glasgow)

Shaw's Dublin City Directory

Smyth, Joseph Constantine, *The Chronicle of the Law Officers of Ireland* (Butterworth, 1839)

Whitaker's Almanack 1931 (Whitaker, 1931)

Who's Who (from 1893)

Primary sources

Ballantine, Mr Serjeant, *Some Experiences of a Barrister's Life* (Richard Bentley, 1883)

British Parliamentary Papers for 1836 and 1853 on Law administration

Carr, Sir Cecil (Ed.), *Pension Books of Clements Inn* (Selden Society, Bernard Quaritch, 1960)

Condon, MM, 'A Wiltshire Sheriff's Notebook 1464–5' in Meekings, CAF, *Medieval English Records* (Devizes Society, 1961)

Doderidge, Thomas, *The English Lawyer* (Assignes of I. More, 1631)

Eddy, JP, *Scarlet and Ermine* (William Kimber, 1960)

Ensor, David, *I Was a Public Prosecutor* (Robert Hale, 1958)

Grierson, Edward, *Confessions of a Country Magistrate* (Victor Gollancz, 1972)

Haggard, H Rider, *A Farmer's Year* (Cresset Library, 1987)

Hastings, Sir Patrick, *Autobiography* (Heinemann, 1948)

Hastings, Sir Patrick, *Cases in Court: a famous barrister's recollections of his most memorable cases* (Macmillan, 1953)

Hawkins, Sir Henry (Baron Brampton), *Reminiscences* (Nelson, 1900)

Humphries, Sir Travers, *Criminal Days* (Hodder and Stoughton, 1946)

Humphries, Sir Travers, *A Book of Trials: personal recollections of an eminent judge of the High Court* (Macmillan, 1956)

Lamb, Charles, *The Essays of Elia* (first published 1820–23) (Routledge, 1920)

McCarthy, Michael, *Five Years in Ireland 1895–1900* (Simpkin, Marshall, Hamilton, Kent, Dublin, 1901)

Neild, Basil, *Farewell to the Assizes: the sixty-one Towns* (Garnstone Press, 1972)

Pettifer, Ernest W, *The Court is Sitting* (Clegg, 1948)

Pinkerton, John M, *The Minute Book of the Faculty of Advocates Vol. 2 1713–1750* (Stair Society, 1980) and Vol. 1 for 1661–1712 (Stair Society, 1976)

Sainty, Sir John, *A List of English Law Officers, King's Counsel and Holders of Patents of Procedure* (Selden, 1987)

Sandbach, JB, *This old Wig: being some recollections of a former London Metropolitan Police Magistrate* (Book Club, 1944)

The Paston Letters (Ed. Norman Davis) (OUP, 1983)

Watson, Robert Patrick, *A Journalist's Experiences of Mixed Society* (Macmillan, 1880)

Secondary works and works cited

Anon. *Mr Punch in Wig and Gown* (Educational Books Co, 1920)

Babington, Anthony, *A House in Bow Street: crime and the magistracy 1740–1881* (Macdonald, 1969)

Baildon, W Paley, *The Quin-Centenary of Lincoln's Inn 1422–1922* (Lincoln's Inn and Country Life, 1923)

Baker, JH, *An Introduction to English Legal History* (Butterworths, 2002)

Baker, JH (Ed.), *The Order of Serjeants-at-Law* (Selden Society, 1984)

Barnard, Sylvia M, *Viewing the Breathless Corpse* (Quacks the printers, 2001)

Bartholomew, Paul C, *The Irish Judiciary* (Institute of Public Administration, Dublin, 1971)

Bevan, Amanda, *Tracing Your Ancestors in The National Archives* (National Archives, 2006)

Birkenhead, Earl of, *Famous Trials* (Hutchinson, 1920)

Birkett, Lord, *Six Great Advocates* (Penguin, 1961)

Birks, M, *Gentlemen of the Law* (Stevens and Sons, 1960)

Birrell, Augustine, *Sir Frank Lockwood: a biographical sketch* (Macmillan, 1898)

Boswell, James, *The Journal of a Tour to the Hebrides* (1773) (Constable, 1906)

Brooks, Christopher, *The Admissions Registers of Barnard's Inn 1620–1869* (Selden Society)

Brown, R Stewart, *Calendar of County Court, City Court and Eyre Rolls of Chester* (Chetham Society, 1925)

Burke, Peter, *The Romance of the Forum* (Hurst and Blackett, 1900)

Burliston, Robert, *Tracing Your Pauper Ancestors* (Pen and Sword, 2009)

Carter, Paul and Thompson, Kate, *Sources for Local Historians* (Phillimore, 2009)

Cheney, CR, *Notaries Public in England* (OUP, 1972)

Cohen, Herman, *A History of the English Bar and Attornatus to 1450* (Sweet and Maxwell, 1929)

Cook, Chris, *The Routledge Companion to Britain in the Nineteenth Century* (Routledge, 2005)

Crawford, Jon G, *A Star Chamber Court in Ireland. The Court of Castle Chamber 1571–1641* (Four Courts, 2006)

Cyriax, Oliver, *The Penguin Encyclopaedia of Crime* (Penguin, 1996)

Daniell, Timothy Tyndale, *The Lawyers – the Inns of Court: the home of the Common Law* (Wildy and Sons, 1976)

Deans, R Storry, *Notable Trials: romances of the law courts* (Cassell, 1906)

Denning, Lord, *Landmarks in the Law* (Butterworths, 1984)

Glazebrook, PR, *Blackstone's Statutes on Criminal Law* (OUP, 2009)

Goodman, Andrew, *The Walking Guide to Lawyers' London* (Blackstone Press, 2000)

Graham, Evelyn, *Fifty years of Famous Judges* (John Long, 1910)

Gregory, Jeremy, and Stevenson, John, *The Routledge Companion to Britain in the Eighteenth Century* (Routledge, 2007)

Hamilton, RG, *All Jangle and Riot: A Barrister's history of the Bar* (Professional Books, 1966)

Hanbury, HG and Yardley, DCM, *English Courts of Law* (OUP, 1979)

Harding, Alan, *A Social History of English Law* (Penguin, 1966)

Harlow, John, *Court Leet Records for the Manor of Manchester in the Sixteenth Century* (Chetham Society, 1864)

Hart, AR, *A History of the King's Serjeants-at-Law in Dublin* (Four Courts Press, 2007)

Herber, Mark, *Legal London: A Pictorial History* (Phillimore, 1999)

Hodge, James H, *Famous Trials* (a series from Penguin Paperbacks) (Various dates from c.1950–60)

Holborn, Guy, *Sources of Biographical Information on Past Lawyers* (British and Irish Association of Law Librarians, 1999)

Hyde, H Montgomery, *Norman Birkett: the life of Lord Birkett of Ulverston* (Hamish Hamilton, 1965)

Irving, Ronald, *The Law is a Ass* (Duckworth, 1999)

Kadri, Sadakat, *The Trial: a history from Socrates to O J Simpson* (Harper, 2006)

Kelly, James, *Poyning's Law and the Making of Law in Ireland 1660–1800* (Four Courts, 2007)

Kingston, Charles, *Famous Judges and Famous Trials* (Stanley Paul, 1910)

Kotsonouris, Mary, *The Winding Up of the Dail Courts* (Four Courts Press, 2004)

Lock, Joan, *Tales from Bow Street* (Robert Hale, 1982)

Manson, Edward, *The Builders of Our Law during the Reign of Queen Victoria* (Horace Cox, 1895)

Meekings, CAF, *Medieval English Records* (Devizes Society, 1961)

Mossman, Mary Jane, *The First Women Lawyers: a comparative study of Gender, Law and the Legal Professions* (Hart Publishing, 2006)

Osborne, Bertram, *Justices of the Peace 1361–1848* (Sedgehill Press, 1959)

Pannick, David, *Judges* (OUP, 1987)

Pannick, David, *Advocates* (OUP, 1992)

Pearsall, Mark, *Family History Companion* (The National Archives, 2007)

Powell, Vincent, *The Legal Companion* (Robson Books, 2005)

Prest, Wilfred R, *The Rise of the Barristers: a social history of the English Bar* (OUP, 1986)

Quinn, AP, *Wigs and Guns: Irish Barristers in the Great War* (Four Courts Press, 2006)

Rede, Thomas Leman, *York Castle* (J Saunders, 1829)

Rivlin, Geoffrey, *Understanding the Law*, (OUP, 2006)

Roughead, William, *Classic Crimes*, edited by Luc Sante (New York Review of Books, 2000)

Saul, Nigel, *A Companion to Medieval England 1066–1485* (Tempus, 2005)

Saunders, John B, *Mozley and Whiteley's Law Dictionary* (Butterworths, 1977)

Seddon, Peter, *The Law's Strangest Cases* (Robson Books, 2005)

Simpson, AWB, *Biographical Dictionary of the Common Law* (Butterworths, 1984)

Sparrow, Gerald, *The Great Judges* (John Long, 1974)

Strahan, JA, *The Bench and Bar of England* (William Blackwood, 1919)

Turner, ES, *May it Please Your Lordship* (Michael Joseph, 1971)

Twiss, Horace, *The Public and Private Life of Lord Chancellor Eldon* (John Murray, 1844)

Whittington-Egan, Richard, *William Roughead's Chronicles of Murder* (Lochar Publishing, 1991)

Woodley, Mick, *Osborn's Concise Law Dictionary* (Sweet and Maxwell, tenth edition, 2005)
Worsfold, T Cato, *Staple Inn and its Story* (Samuel Bagster, 1903)
Wright, S Fowler, *The Life of Sir Walter Scott* (Poetry League, 1932)

Scottish and Irish: Specific Surveys

For Scotland, David Moody's *Scottish Family History* in the Batsford Local History Series (1988), is an excellent starting point and a very useful reference work for all aspects of the subject. For Ireland, Ian Maxwell's *How to Trace Your Irish Ancestors* (How To, 2008) has a very useful section on law and order. Both provide readable explanations of the particular elements of the national history which impinge on the lawyers' records.

Related Family History Publications

Brooks, Brian and Herber, Mark, *My Ancestor was a Lawyer* (Genealogical Society, 2006)
Gibson, Jeremy and Rogers, Colin, *Coroners' Records in England and Wales* (Federation of Family History Societies, 2005)

Magazines, Newspapers and Periodicals

Ancestors
Criminal Law Review
Dublin Historical Record
Eastern Morning News
Freeman's Journal
Gentleman's Magazine
Hedon History Newsletter
Journal of Legal History
Journal of Social History
Juridical Review
Justice of the Peace
Law Notes: a monthly magazine
Strand magazine

The Irish Jurist
The Local Historian
The Times Digital Archive
Times Literary Supplement
T.P.'s Weekly

Articles

Note: a visit to a university library which teaches law will provide all kinds of legal publications of use, notably the printed reports under *All England Law Reports,* and also earlier journals which no longer exist, such as *The Criminal Law Review.* See also *Ancestors* issue 59, 'Begging for Mercy'. This relates to the Home Office records regarding petitions and pleas for mercy. It expands the references made to HO47 at page 78.

Auchmuty, Rosemary, 'Early Women Law Students at Cambridge and Oxford', *Journal of Legal History* Vol.29 No.1 April, 2008 pp.63–97

Baker, JH, 'Lawyers Practising in Chancery 1474–1486', *Journal of Legal History* pp.54–57, 1994

Cairns, John W, 'The Origins of the Edinburgh Law School, the Union of 1707 and the Regius Chair', *Edinburgh Law Review,* Sept. 2007

Clarke, Keith C, 'The Justice's Clerk', *Criminal Law Review* 1964 pp.620–33

Ferguson, Kenneth, 'The Irish Bar in December, 1798', *Dublin Historical Record* Vol. 52 No.1 (Spring, 1999) pp.32–60

Finlay, John, 'Pettyfoggers, Regulation and Local Courts in Early Modern Scotland', *The Scottish Historical Review* Vol. LXXXVII No. 223 April 2008 pp.42–67

Gibb, Frances, 'Judges put on trial to test their courtroom skills', *The Times* 1.9.09 p.19

Gibb, Frances, 'Written tests are no guide to your ability to be a judge', *The Times* 29.1.09 p. 59

Jennings, Paul, 'Liquor Licensing and the Local Historian: the 1904 Licensing Act', *The Local Historian* Vol. 39 No. 1 Feb. 2009 pp.48–61

King, Peter, 'The Summary Courts and Social Relations in Eighteenth Century England', *Past and Present* No. 183 May 2004 pp.125–172

Pannick, David, 'From Lay Peers to Supreme Court Judges', *The Times*, 30.7.09 p.50

Slinn, Judy, *Freshfield Family*, Entry in the *Oxford Dictionary of National Biography*

Websites

A good place to start in order to appreciate the sheer extent and depth of legal historical organisations is the gateway site from the Faculty of Law at the University of Cambridge. This is at www.law.cam.ac.uk/resources_history.php Here, there are to be found links to legal history groups, and also resources listed by period and topic, such as Anglo Saxon/Medieval/Early Common Law/feudalism etc. There are links to major archives here as well, for instance to the Institute of Historical Research and Tarlton Law Library at Texas, which has substantial resources. More specifically for family history, there are links to counties, such as to the Lincolnshire Eyre of 1202 or the Staffordshire Eyre of 1203. Arching over all this is the Index of Resources for Historians (University of Kansas).

As a generally useful support, it is worth checking the publications lists of publishers who specialise in legal history in the United Kingdom and in the Republic of Ireland. An outstanding example of this is the series on Irish Legal History from the Four Courts Press in Dublin.

www.aalt.law.uh.edu
www.barcouncil.org.uk/about/history
www.batchmates.com/bmtimes/content
www.blacksheepindex.co.uk
www.britannia.com/history/coroner
www.british-history.ac.uk/source
www.chambersandpartners.com
www.cliffordelmerbooks.com
www.coronersociety.org.uk
www.dur.ac.uk/surtees.society/History1

www.ehow.co.uk/about
www.exclassics.com/newgate/ngintro.htm
www.ffhs.org.uk
www.fourcourtspress.ie/subcategory.php
www.ireland-information.com/reference/legalsys.html
www.irishtimes.com/ancestor/browse/records/news/indexes.htm
www.lawreports.co.uk
www.lawscot.org.uk/about
www.lexisnexis.org.uk
www.local-history.co.uk
www.nas.gov.uk/guides/justice.asp
www.public-prism.qub.ac.uk/TalisPrism/doSearch.do
www.scriveners.org.uk
www.stairsociety.org/links.htm
www.thegenealogist.co.uk
www.thewssociety.co.uk/index.asp
www.ukcle.ac.uk/resources/scotland/context.html
www.vcp.e2bn.org
www.welshlegalhistory.org

For the website relating to the *Oxford Dictionary of National Biography*, see www.oxforddnb.com/templates/theme and this will have a list of themes, one of which is the law resource. Judy Slinn's article on the Freshfield company is cross-referenced there also.

Official website of the UK Judiciary

www.parliament.uk/judicial_work.cfm
www.privy-council.org.uk

Organisations

Not all of these organisations will have records of lawyers; some sites will include lists but other will not. There are also some sites of organisations which concentrate on other aspects of crime and justice but which will have marginal holdings which will be of use.

The Bar Council
189–193 High Holborn
London
WC1V 7HZ

The Bar Council of Northern Ireland
31 Chichester Street
Belfast
BT1 3JQ

British Association for Local History
PO Box 6549
Somersal Herbert
Ashbourne
DE6 5WH

Institute of Legal Executives
Kempston Manor
Kempston
Bedford
MK42 7AB

The Irish Legal History Society
Department of Law
Trinity College Dublin
Arts Building
Dublin 2
Eire

The Law Society
The Law Society's Hall
113 Chancery Lane
London
WC2A 1PL

The Law Society of Ireland
Blackhall Place

Dublin 7
Ireland

The Law Society of Scotland
26 Drumsheugh Gardens
Edinburgh
EH3 7YR

Linen Hall Library
17 Donegal Square North
Belfast
BT1 5GD

National Library of Ireland
Kildare Street
Dublin 2
Eire

National Library of Wales
Aberystwyth
Ceredigion
Wales
SY23 2BU

Public Record Office of Northern Ireland
66 Balmoral Avenue
Belfast
BT9 6NY

The Secretary
The Selden Society
School of Law
Queen Mary
Mile End Road
London
E1 4NS

The Society of Legal Scholars
School of Law
University of Southampton
Southampton
SO17 1BJ

The Stair Society
6 The Glebe
Manse Road
Dirleton
East Lothian
EH39 5FB

(The Stair Society website has a large number of links to other kindred groups)

The Surtees Society
Faculty Office
Elvet Riverside Block 2
New Elvet
Durham
DH1 3JT

Welsh Legal History Society
School of Law
Bangor University
Gwynedd
LL57 2DG

Writers to the Signet
Signet Library
Parliament Square
Edinburgh
EH1 1RF

INDEX

Williams, Montagu, 96, 111
Later Leaves, 101
Wood, Jane, 118
Worsfold, T Cato, 38–9
Worshipful Company of
    Scriveners, 115

Writer to the Signet, 139–41
Wynne, Watkins, 84

Year Books, 22–3
York Minster, 97